The Loud Halo

The Loud Halo

LILLIAN BECKWITH

A COMMON READER EDITION
THE AKADINE PRESS

The Loud Halo

A COMMON READER EDITION published 1998
by The Akadine Press, Inc., by arrangement with the author.

A COMMON READER EDITION and fountain colophon are trademarks
of The Akadine Press, Inc.

ISBN 1-888173-52-1

2 4 6 8 10 9 7 5 3

To:
Ealasaid & Goiridh

Vocabulary

Bodach	Old man
Burn	A fast-flowing river or brook
Byre	A cowshed
Cailleach	Old woman
Ceilidh	A meeting for gossip and song
Cleg	A species of horse-fly
Crack	A gossipy chat
Croft	A very small farm
Crowdie	An unpressed cheese made from sour milk
Ealasaid	Elizabeth
Fly cuppie	A cup of tea snatched between meals
Girdle	A round metal plate for baking scones
Graipe	A fork for digging
He breeah!	It is fine!
Mo ghaoil	My dear
Mucking	Cleaning out
Pliachs	A wooden implement for making holes when planting potatoes
Shingle	A stony shore
Skelpings	A slapping or thrashing
Sneck	A door latch
Sprackle	An apparently aimless wandering
Stook	A large haycock
Strupak	A cup of tea and a bite to eat
Tackety	A boot sole studded with tacks
Tatties	Potatoes
Tigh	A house
Tingles	Metal patches on the hull of a boat
Truckling	Yielding

Contents

The Loud Halo

I. *Johnny Comic*

THE STORM-FORCE WIND was blasting squalls of incredibly wet and heavy rain across the loch, blotting out the hills and the sky and flaying the rusty grass of the crofts until it cringed back into the ground from which it had sprung so ebulliently only a few short months earlier. All day there had been semi-dusk and when I had returned soaked and shivering from the moors that morning after a long hunt to give Bonny her morning hay, I had promised myself I would do nothing but change into dry clothes, put some food on a tray and then sit by the fire with a book. Nothing, that is, until it was time for me to don my sticky oilskins and my coldly damp sou'wester, strain on wet gumboots and go seeking Bonny again with her evening feed.

There was no doubt Bruach cows were hardy creatures, and it took hardy humans to live up to them. Left to roam the treeless, craggy moors for nine months of the year the cattle had to seek shelter where they could from the fierce winds, lashing hail, rain and even snow which beset the Hebrides from about September onwards. The cows, being wise creatures, could be relied upon to find it. The humans, being not so wise, were not nearly so reliable. So, with a milk pail in one hand, a stick in the other, a sack of hay roped to our backs, we plodded the thousands of acres of moor, more often than not in combat with a gale-force wind that hurled stinging rain into our faces. Panting and praying, we climbed up rocks with the intention of gaining a better view; dejected and swearing, we wallowed in bogs with no intention at all.

I use the plural pronoun because on the surface this was what we all appeared to do, but I suspect privately that I, being an acolyte, was the only one who was really exasperated by the weather, by the cantankerousness of the cows or by the time it all took. The rest of the crofters knew their weather better, they knew their moors better and, in the short days of winter, time to them was only a hiatus between getting up and the evening ceilidh and they had no particular preference as to how they helped it along.

'But why don't you put bells on the cattle like they do in Switzerland?' asked a woman tourist to whom I once described our sufferings. It was easy to discern that she was dreaming pleasant dreams of 'a little cottage in the Highlands and a cow for milk' when she retired. It was then an evening of summer calm when the protesting cry of a disturbed heron seemed to stab the night with its volume and one could almost hear the whisper of gulls' wings as they dawdled homeward.

'It wouldn't work here,' I told her. 'The wind's far too strong in winter. You wouldn't be able to hear a peal of church bells here in a good gale.'

'But surely if you had a telescope you could just climb the highest hill and then you could see all round.'

She made it sound so easy and I tried to explain to her how impossible it would be for anyone, burdened with hay, to climb the highest hill and then to hold a telescope in the teeth of a gale and that even a telescope won't bend and look down into innumerable secret corries.

I recognized in her remarks the suspicion a stranger is so apt to form on first acquaintance with the Hebrides— that the crofter prefers to make life difficult for himself and that he has built-in resistance to progress. But experience had taught me there was no other way to keep a self-willed Highland cow in a village where crofts were traditionally unfenced, hay was almost as traditionally scarce and where the cows themselves were as suspicious of a bowl of concentrates as they might be of a bowl of hot cinders. The majority of them tolerated only three additions to their heather and hay diet: a 'potach', which is scalded oatmeal pressed into a ball; a bowl of boiled potatoes dried off with oatmeal; or a bowl of boiled seaweed mashed up with salt herring and dried off with oatmeal. As you could always smell out the kitchen of a crofter who fed his cows on this last delicacy Bonny never got the chance to try it. I had once tried to ingratiate myself with her by buying a bag of turnips and offering them to her at first whole, then chopped up in a bowl and sprinkled with oatmeal, and then, desperately, piece by piece in my fingers. She merely blew her nose over them and me and I formed the opinion then that there can be few creatures in the world that can express disdain so sublimely as a Highland cow. I offered the remaining turnips round the village but neither the cows nor the humans evinced any interest whatever.

'Not even that queer beastie of Kirsty's will so much as look at them,' reported Morag, 'an' yon's the one will eat chocolate cake and jam sandwiches and oranges if she'll get the chance.'

Morag and I shared the rest of the turnips between us and ate them ourselves.

I was thinking of all these things as I put on dry clothes, poured out a plate of soup, drew my chair close to the fire and put my book in readiness on the table. As I turned to sit down my eye caught an unexpected flicker of movement through the salt-encrusted window, and dreading that it was part of the byre roof or hen house blowing away I hurried to peer out.

'Oh blast!' I exclaimed as the movement resolved itself into the wind-flapped edge of a man's overcoat. I had lulled myself into thinking that the malevolence of the day would have ensured for me an afternoon of complete privacy but I had forgotten that there was one man who was completely undeterred from his ramblings whatever the weather. 'Oh well,' I thought resignedly, 'better him than to see the byre roof taking off, I suppose.'

Johnny Comic came in through the gate and turned to shut it, patting it tenderly as though telling it, as he would a dog, to stay there quietly until he returned. This curious tenderness for everything, animate or inanimate, was typical of Johnny and he would no more have dreamed of hurting the feelings of a gate by rushing through it and slamming it after him than he would have of hurting the feelings of a friend by refusing to acknowledge a greeting. He was a strange-looking man, so oddly shaped it looked as if his mother might have made him herself from a 'do-it-yourself' kit and that he had then blundered rather than grown into manhood. He was slightly built, his legs being disproportionately long and hampered with large feet like road shovels; one leg was longer than the other so that it dragged as he walked. His arms were short, while great hands with thick fingers hung from them like bunches of bananas. His eyes were the guileless blue of childhood; his skin pale and smooth as a woman's, and the grey curls around his head were soft and fine as the seed-head of a dandelion. Indeed, one felt one needed only to puff once, twice, perhaps three times, to disperse them all.

I opened the door to him and he stood on the threshold smiling broadly, confident of his welcome, while the kitchen door slammed with a vehemence that juddered all the china on the dresser.

'My, but it's coarse, coarse weather,' he paused to say politely before he stepped inside, despite the fact that the rain was sluicing in through the open door and the wind had whipped the hall pictures into a frenzy of swinging and was now wrapping the wet doormat around my legs.

'Go into the fire quickly, Johnny,' I urged, smothering my exasperation as I leaned hard on the door to shut it against the bullying rush of the wind.

He writhed out of his top layer of clothing, which comprised various pieces of oilskin of assorted shapes, and threw them down on the stairs. Still murmuring faint comments on the weather he wandered into the kitchen, pulled my chair away from the fire where I had placed it and sat himself down.

'I'll make a wee strupak as soon as I've had my soup,' I told him, and sat down opposite him. It was no use offering Johnny soup, that I knew, for his diet was restricted to a plate of porridge and three hard-boiled eggs. For each one of his three meals, every day, it was the same, varying only when he took a 'wee strupak' with neighbours, when he would permit himself a piece of girdle scone with jam. He ate neither meat nor vegetables, nor even bread and butter. I was staggered when he had first told me and had sought confirmation from others who knew him.

'Aye, and it's right enough,' they told me. 'Ever since he was old enough to take it that's all he's lived on.' Which made me suspect that death for Johnny, like Peter Pan, 'Would be an awfully great adventure.'

As I ate my soup I watched Johnny, who had extracted a piece of wood from deep in his pocket and was whittling away at it inexpertly with a knife that I knew from experience was as blunt as a stick of rhubarb, and pondered on why he, specifically, had been dubbed 'Comic', a label which

I felt could have been much more aptly bestowed on so many other inhabitants of the village. No one seemed to know how he had come by it. Old men, drawing the 'pension', recalled that even in his schooldays he had been 'Johnny Comic' to schoolmaster and scholars alike.

'He was always the clown, was Johnny,' they invariably added, 'and he took in no learning save what the schoolmaster leathered in through the seat of his breeks.'

I had first met Johnny the day I moved into my own cottage in Bruach when, as soon as the furniture had been carried in and the willing helpers had left to attend to their cattle, he had suddenly appeared outside the window, where he had settled himself, elbows resting comfortably on the sill, and had subjected me to an embarrassing mute scrutiny as I wrestled with a reluctant stove and endeavoured in the midst of chaos to cook myself a meal. When I appeared to be looking for something he would peer anxiously into the room, pressing his face against the glass. When I seemed to have found whatever I was looking for he would grin and nod with satisfaction. He did not live in the village and I had never seen him before but eventually for both our sakes I called him to come inside; for a moment his expression was one of horror and then he almost fell in his anxiety to get away from the window. By the time I had reached the door he was hurrying across the moor as fast as he could go.

'Ach, but mo ghaoil, he'll not be knowin' you and he'd be frightened likely that you'd seduct him. The lads tease him, the wretches,' Morag explained when I told her of the incident.

Once I was settled in my cottage Johnny, apparently having no more fear of or less aversion to losing his pudicity, got over his mistrust of me and became a regular visitor. Every couple of weeks he would walk to Bruach over the moor, his awkward shambling gait seeming to carry him rapidly across country in all kinds of weather without any sign of distress. He came, as he explained, because he thought I'd like a ceilidh, but his real reason for visiting me, though it was never allowed to emerge until towards the end of his stay, was to sell me some small article he had made and thereby earn a few coppers for 'wootpines', for he loved a clandestine smoke and his sister Kirsty, with whom he lived, appropriated all his pension. Sometimes it would be a small model boat made from driftwood, sometimes a glass netfloat in a piece of herring net, but more often than not it would be a heather besom. The frequency with which he offered me these indeed suggested that he himself had little faith in the lasting quality of his handiwork; if he ever noticed the ingenious windbreak I contrived of upended besoms he never commented on it.

I brewed tea, spread some pieces of scone with jam and put them beside him on the table. Then I made some excuse to go upstairs. My first attempts to entertain Johnny had been embarrassing for both of us. I had poured out a cup of tea and placed it beside him along with a plate of scones. He had sugared the tea and stirred it, wiping the spoon carefully on his coat sleeve before replacing it in the basin. All the time I was drinking my own tea he had talked politely, never so much as glancing at his own cup so that it had got quite cold. I had offered to empty his cup and refill it with hot tea and he had accepted with alacrity. Once again he had repeated the ritual of sugaring it and wiping the spoon, but despite my urgings he had again left it to go cold, and still had not touched the scones. Feeling a little piqued I had filled his cup yet again with hot tea and then quite without design I had gone to get something from the shed. When I returned after only a very brief interval the tea had disappeared and so had all the scones. The next time he came much the same thing had happened but by the time he paid his third visit I knew what was expected of me and obliged accordingly.

When I came downstairs after a discreetly judged interval Johnny had finished his strupak and was leaning back in the chair.

'More tea or scone, Johnny?' I offered.

'No, thank you, I've done lovely,' he replied, lifting one of his large hands in a gesture of repression. He waited expectantly until from the dresser I reached down a jar of baking-soda and a spoon which I kept especially for Johnny. Avidly he dug in the spoon and with obvious relish swallowed three or four heaped spoonfuls of the powder, spilling it down his jersey in his eagerness to get the spoon into his mouth. Then he replaced the jar on the table, dusted down the front of his jersey and leaned back in his chair to stare tranquilly at the ceiling and to remain splendidly indifferent to his own loud and fulsome belchings which when I had first heard them had filled me with consternation but which now I accepted with only slight uneasiness. Once,

11

thinking I was doing Johnny a good turn, I had refused the baking-soda, but when I had returned to the kitchen the trail of white powder from the dresser to Johnny's chair had told its own tale and I was so ashamed of myself for causing the look of guilt on Johnny's normally ingenuous face that I never had the heart to refuse again.

The belchings diminished in volume and I started to move about the kitchen, wishing that Johnny would realize that it would soon be dusk and that I had yet to go and milk my cow. It was unthinkable that the solicitous 'Ach, but I'm keeping you back', which is the polite Bruach way of telling a stranger it is high time he went, should be used by an English woman to a Gael. I groped for an alternative. On the dresser was a bowl of peanuts still in their shells which had been sent to me from England. Taking a good handful I put them into a bag and offered them to Johnny.

'Take these home to Kirsty,' I said.

Johnny turned them over suspiciously. 'Which is these?' he asked me.

'They're peanuts,' I told him. 'Very good to eat.'

He still continued to turn them between his large fingers.

'I'm taking some with me to chew while I'm looking for the cow.'

'Aye?' he agreed uncertainly. He put them in his pocket and went through into the hall where I heard him struggling into his jigsaw of oilskins. I rushed out of the back door to get meal for Bonny's potach and to collect the milk pail. When I came back into the kitchen Johnny met me with an approving smile.

'Them things is good, good,' he asserted.

'What things?' I asked stupidly, my mind on the task ahead.

'Them nuts, you say. They're good I'm tellin' you.'

'Oh, have you eaten some? I thought you'd like them,' I said. 'Here take some more to eat on your way home.' I took another handful from the bowl. 'Give me your bag and I'll fill it up,' I said, anxious to hurry him on his way so that I might look for Bonny without the dubious assistance of a torch. He proffered me an empty bag. 'Have you eaten them all, Johnny?' I asked, mildly astonished.

'Aye, an' they was good I'm sayin'.'

I dribbled more nuts into his bag. 'You'd better give me the shells and I'll throw them into the fire,' I said. 'Otherwise Kirsty will be complaining that I encourage you to fill your pockets with rubbish.'

'Shells?' he repeated vaguely.

'Yes, the shells off the peanuts. Have you thrown them away, then?' I glanced down at the floor hoping he had not scattered them at random as he did his wood chippings.

'These has shells?' he demanded, taking one from the bag and holding it up.

'Why, yes, of course,' I began to explain. 'Look,' and then I broke off to stare at him with mounting concern. 'Johnny, you didn't eat the shells too,' I accused.

'I eat them,' retorted Johnny proudly. 'I eat all of them

13

an' they're good, I'm tellin' you.' With great bravado he popped a couple of nuts into his mouth and chewed them noisily.

'But, Johnny,' I remonstrated, 'you mustn't eat the shells. They'll give you terrible indigestion!'

Completely unperturbed he continued to pop nuts into his mouth, still chewing with gusto. 'Never have indigestion in my life,' he assured me happily.

'Never had indigestion!' I exclaimed. 'Then why on earth do you take all that baking-soda?'

For a moment he looked vaguely perplexed, and then, wagging a finger at me, he recommended: 'Take plenty bakin'-sody and never no indigestion. Just plenty sody.'

I opened the door and the wind charged in. Johnny met it with a magnificent belch which had such a repelling effect that in the brief respite I managed to slam the door behind him.

'Thank you for that, Johnny,' I murmured with a smile and went to the task of getting into my gumboots and oilskins once again.

II. *Matters Marine*

HECTOR HAD DECIDED to sell his boat *Wayfarer* so that he could buy a bigger one with more accommodation for passengers, for Bruach was being discovered by a steadily increasing number of campers and coach tourists and the crofters were confidently predicting that the coming season would be a bumper one. Some days after his advertisement had appeared in a Highland paper Hector turned up at my cottage with a sheaf of letters he had received in reply.

'It's a grand day,' he proffered with beguilement in his blue eyes and a diffidence in his voice that was no doubt induced by the fact that it was at least six weeks since our last meeting and that I had, on that occasion, soundly upbraided him for daring to borrow my one and only toothbrush. He had been bewildered and hurt by my attack and had been quick to assure me that he had put the brush back most carefully in its tumbler beside the water bucket where it was always kept. What he hadn't been able to reassure me about was why, when I came to use the toothbrush, its bristles should have been fuzzy with black hair that was exactly the same shade and texture as his own.

'Why, Hector!' I greeted him now with genuine cordiality, for no one could help loving him whatever he did, 'where on earth have you been all this time? I don't seem to have seen you for ages.'

'Ach, I'm just where the tide left me when last you saw me,' he said with a gloomy smile. I told him to sit down but he remained standing, shuffling from one foot to another and gnawing along the length of a grubby forefinger.

'Behag was tellin' me,' he began, and then pushing up his peaked cap he rubbed an exploratory hand among the sparse hair it constrained. 'I was wonderin',' he started again, this time pulling at his ear, 'maybe would you do me a few wee letters on tsat machine you have? I'm tsinkin' it would be quicker.'

I looked up from the sewing machine on which I was running up a pair of gay new curtains. 'Of course I'll do them,' I agreed. 'Do you want them right away?'

'Ach, no.' With renewed confidence he drew up a chair and sat down beside me. 'You can finish what you're doin' first,' he told me magnanimously.

I turned back to the machine.

'Will I work the handle for you,' he offered when he had watched me long enough to be sure the task required very little exertion. I said that I would prefer to do it myself and while I put on a new reel of cotton and re-threaded the needle he toyed delightedly with the material, rubbing it between his stained fingers and examining the bright red peonies with which it was patterned. 'Tsese is nice flowers,' he confided. 'I mind they used to call tsem "chrissie-annies" in Glasgow when I was tsere.'

When I commenced sewing again Hector bent over me anxiously. Now despite the fact that I need to wear spectacles for close work I flatter myself that I can run up a straight seam as neatly as anyone, but Hector, who admittedly had perfect eyesight, was so dubious of my skill that every few inches if he considered there was the slightest deviation he would give an audible 'tech' of concern and an enthusiastic twitch at the material, which resulted in the sewing of a pronounced 'V'. I must confess I was too amused to curb his enthusiasm though by the time I had reached the end of the seam the stitching resembled a wavering flight of birds. I thought it might be more satisfactory if I finished the curtains when I was alone but he was insistent that the work should not be put aside just for his 'few wee letters'. I suspected that he was thoroughly enjoying guiding what he no doubt believed to be my very erratic hand, and he seemed greatly disappointed when we had finished and I announced that I must press the curtains before they were hung so that he would have to wait until his next visit before he could admire the full effect of his collaboration.

I put away the sewing machine and brought out the typewriter. 'Now,' I invited, when there was a sheet of paper in the machine, 'tell me what you want to say.'

He began to chew his finger again. 'Well, what will I tell tsem?' he demanded perplexedly.

'What do you want to tell them?' I retaliated.

He put the letters down on the table beside me. 'Well, tsat one wants to know is tse engine forrard or aft. You could tell him it's aft.' He brought up one of his knees and attempted to rub his chin on it. 'Tsere's anusser wants to know where is tse wheelhouse. You can tell tsem it's aft too.' He sat back limp and exhausted.

I glanced quickly through the letters. 'They all want to know the price you're asking. You'll need to give them an idea of that,' I told him.

Hector looked momentarily discomfited. He did not want me or anyone else in the village to know the price he had set on *Wayfarer*. 'Well, now, I'll not be knowin' what to ask for her,' he prevaricated. 'Behag's sayin' one tsing and tse cailleach's sayin' anusser.'

'We'll leave that blank then, and you can fill it in when you and Behag have decided,' I suggested.

'Aye, aye. Tsat'll be tse way of it.' He cheered up instantly.

I drew up a list of questions and asked Hector for the answers. 'Now,' I told him. 'We'll just set down all this information in each letter and then they'll know as much about the boat as you can tell them. Is that all right?'

'Tsat's fine,' said Hector.

'Shall I just begin, "Dear Sir, In reply to your letter of such and such a date, here is the information you ask for. . . ."?'

'We cannot say "Dear Sir",' cut in Hector with shocked disapproval. 'Not when you're writin' to folks about a boat.'

'Why not?' I asked with surprise. 'You don't know these people, so you should begin with "Dear Sir".'

'It's no' friendly,' he argued.

'It's perfectly correct,' I insisted.

'Ach, no,' he said, fidgeting with embarrassment at having to argue with me. 'As like as not tsey won't even read it if you say tsat.'

'Why ever shouldn't they, Hector?' I demanded, my voice edged with asperity.

Hector frowned. 'Well, if ever I get a letter and it begins with "Dear Sir" then I throw it straightway into the fire because I know it'll be a nasty one,' he explained.

Together we pondered the assortment of letters, deciphering names and addressing them in as friendly a manner as Hector wished and also, at his insistence, we informed the prospective buyers chattily that in Bruach it had been a very coarse winter; that the potatoes would surely be very late going into the ground this year and that the Department of Agriculture bull had arrived earlier than expected. Hector then professed himself completely satisfied. 'I'll put a P.S. at tse end tellin' tsem tse price,' he said with true Gaelic finesse.

A month went by; a month of exhilarating dawns which heralded days that stretched themselves to hold more and more hours of gentle sunshine. The seared wintry grass of the crofts took on a more comely appearance and wherever one's glance rested there were bursting buds and courting birds and all the lovely lilting things of spring. Old men in creased dark clothes came out of their winter hiding places and leaned against the walls of the houses, sampling the quality of the sunlight and pronouncing upon the condition of the cattle, upon the prospects of the fishing, or, if encouraged, upon the fate of the world. The children left off their tackety boots and thick hand-knit socks and skipped to school barefooted with the same friskiness as the young lambs bleating on the hills, while on the dry, heathery moors the local incendiarists, with whom every village in the Islands seems to be afflicted, wantonly satisfied their urges so that there was rarely a day when one did not see the spreading blue tendrils of heather smoke creeping steadily or tillering and racing menacingly according to the whim of the wind.

For all of us the days were full of the outdoors: cutting peats, turning them, lifting and finally stacking them; burning the unruly patches of sedge that no scythe could master; gathering up the stones which always seemed to stray on to the crofts during the winter of neglect; teaching new calves to drink from a pail while one stroked the sun-warmed curls of its back and endured the caress of a milky tongue. For the women there was in addition the annual blanket washing, perhaps in a zinc bath of water carried laboriously pailful by pailful from the well, perhaps in a cauldron over a wood fire beside the burn. We worked dedicatedly, cramming the days with toil, and when dusk approached and we could feel we had earned a respite we walked to our homes with the clean cool wind from the hill fanning our glowing faces and our bodies heavy with that good weariness that comes from physical labour in the open air.

It was after just such a day that I went out to do my last chore of the evening. The sun had not long set in a splendour of vermilion and turquoise and the sky was still streaked as though it had been clawed by gory fingernails. Busy ripples flecked with silver raced across the loch and tumbled with Dresden tinkles on to the pebbles of the shore. The hills looked smug and withdrawn behind a faint veil of mist while across the water the brightest of the lighthouses was already beginning to show as a dim spark on the horizon. My line of newly washed blankets, now dry and wind softened, stirred lazily and as I unpegged each one I did it lingeringly and with a feeling of ecstasy as though I might be dipping a flag in salute to the glory of the night.

'Here! Come an' get me a drink of water. My hands is all sticky!' Erchy's voice, uneasy with authority, came from the direction of the house. Obediently, I gathered up the blankets and went indoors. Erchy was holding a large brush in front of him, its bristles sticky with glistening tar. His hands too were liberally coated. 'I'm that thirsty I'm like to faint,' he told me.

I dumped the blankets on the table well out of his way and poured out a large mug of water. He drank it with audible relish but when I offered to make tea for him he declined it.

'I didn't take my dinner yet,' he explained. (In Bruach one always 'took' one's meals.)

'Then you must be hungry. Let me give you a scone or something.'

'I daren't wait,' he insisted. 'See, I promised the cailleach I'd see to the cow for her tonight as she's goin' ceilidhin' over with Katy. She'll be makin' a swear at me already for bein' as late as I am.' He leaned his elbow on the dresser. 'She wasn't for lettin' me come down here today at all but I told her I'd get the boat tarred while she was good and dry.'

'Tar!' I repeated with a grimace of disgust. 'Why is it you always put so much tar on your boats? Why don't you paint them in nice bright colours instead of just slathering them with dirty black tar?'

Erchy appeared slightly outraged. 'Tar keeps out the water better than paint,' he defended. 'Any splits in the planks or any places where she might be takin' in the water, once they're filled with tar they'll keep out the sea for as long as the season lasts,' he explained.

'I'd like to think there was something more than a gob of tar between me and the sea,' I murmured.

'Ach!' snorted Erchy.

'Anyway it doesn't alter the fact that it's unsightly stuff,' I told him.

'Damty sure it is,' agreed Erchy amiably. 'Here,' he demanded. 'D'you mind Tarry Ruari?'

I shook my head. 'No,' I replied. 'I've seen the house where he lived but he was dead when I came here.'

'You've seen his house? Then you'll know the way it's tarred all over—the roof and the walls—all black?'

I remembered Ruari's house as a stained hovel of a place near a boggy slope of the burn and recalled Morag describing it as being 'very delaborated'.

'Yes,' I admitted, 'it did look as if it might have been tarred.'

'Now that's a man went mad with tar,' said Erchy with complete seriousness. 'He tarred his wee boat inside and out over and over again until she was that heavy he could hardly pull her up the beach. Then he started tarring his house—outside at first and then on the inside. He even tarred the furniture. By God! but you never saw such a place in your life. Folks here just used to laugh at him at first but then the nurse went there one day and found he'd tarred the blankets on his bed. They came and took him away then.'

'Good gracious!' I ejaculated. 'Was he married?'

'Oh, no,' explained Erchy simply. 'Just daft.'

He moved vaguely towards the door. 'I'd best be goin',' he said. 'Thanks for the drink. I was badly needin' it.'

'I'm sorry it wasn't something more sustaining,' I told him with spurious apology.

Erchy turned quickly. 'Indeed but I wouldn't have thanked you for it just now, then.'

'No?' I mocked.

'Damty sure I wouldn't. If you'd handed me a bottle of whisky I would have given it back to you without a thought for it.'

'I'd like to see you refuse whisky,' I said.

'Well, you will someday at that.'

I smiled disbelievingly.

'You know,' he went on, 'I reckon that's the reason folks like me don't go bad with the drink like they do in Glasgow and them places. You see what I mean?'

I waited, not at all sure that I did.

'What I'm sayin' is, take me at the cattle sale. I've plenty of money on me so I get drunk as hell on it for maybe two or three days. Well, then I come to the end of it and I don' want anything but to get out on to the hill. I make an excuse to go after the sheep and I'm away first light without my breakfast and only a wee potach in my pocket. When I get thirsty I put my head down into one of the burns—the colder the better—and I can tell you it's sweet! When I've had one drink I'm lookin' forward to tastin' the water in the next place and the next. By the time I come back again I feel as though I never want to take a drop of whisky again in my life.'

'But it doesn't last?' I queried.

'No, thank God,' said Erchy fervently. He appeared to muse for a few moments before he spoke again. 'Did I tell you I'm a big sheep man now?' he asked, changing the subject completely.

'No,' I said. 'Since when?'

'I found them up on the hill one time when I was away like I've been tellin' you.'

'Found them?' I echoed.

'Aye, as true as I'm here.'

'How long have they been lost?'

'Well, it was about five years ago now that I was takin' some old ewes that I had to the sale and one of them went lame on the way so I drove her off to the side of the road and left her there. There was no sign of her by the time I got back so I never gave her another thought except that she'd probably go off somewhere quiet and die. The beasts was only worth a few bob then, anyway. Well, like I was sayin', I was up there on the hill and in a wee corrie all by themselves I came on an old ewe and a ram, two sheep and three young lambs. I caught the ewe first an' there was my markings on her. I had the dog with me so I caught the rest of them an' they had no markings on them at all so I knew they must be mine. She would have been in lamb when I left her,' he explained, 'an' it must have been a ram lamb.'

'It's strange no one has noticed them before,' I said.

'Ach, no, not where they was,' he told me. 'Nobody goes much round the back of the Beinn there, an' the corrie they was in you wouldn't see from the path. That old ewe's a hardy, though,' he muttered appreciatively, 'she hadn't as much fleece left on her as you'd need to bait a hook.' He made another vague move towards the door but in his reminiscent mood I knew he would linger for another half-hour at least before he finally detached himself from the cottage, so I began preparing my evening meal.

'It must be very pleasant to come across a flock of sheep you didn't know you had,' I remarked as I grated cheese into a basin.

Erchy watched me curiously. 'Aye,' he admitted. He

came back to the table. 'What's that you're makin'?'

'Oh, just a cheese sauce,' I told him.

'I mind fine when my sister was at home—she's a cook in Edinburgh, you know, and she has to make these fancy things there—she found some cheese in the cupboard that had gone dry. Ach, I can eat the stuff in the winter all right but not in the summer when there's plenty of crowdie,' he explained hurriedly. 'She handed me one of those grater things and told me to get on and grate it for her. Hell, by the time I'd finished all my fingernails had gone into the basin, too. When I showed her she was mad at me so I told her she wasn't to make me do it for her again,' he finished with remembered triumph. I opened a bottle and poured a little of its contents into the pan. Erchy sniffed.

'That's beer!' he accused. 'I thought you didn't like it?'

'I don't like to drink it,' I said. 'But I do sometimes use it in sauces.'

'I wouldn't fancy beer like that,' he said, shaking his head. 'Now if it was whisky. . . .'

'There you go again,' I taunted. 'You're obsessed with whisky.'

'No, not me,' he denied. 'I like to have a good drink when I have one but that's only when I have the money. I'm not like these folks from Rudha that has a bottle sent out on the bus two or three times every week.'

'Tell me, Erchy,' I asked, for he had touched on a subject that had been puzzling me for a long time, 'how do they manage to afford bottles of whisky two or three times a week? They're only crofters and some of them even draw

Public Assistance, yet they seem to be able to buy drink and cigarettes as much as ever they want to. They don't seem to go short of anything.'

'No, an' I'm damty sure they never will,' said Erchy, looking mysterious.

'What's their secret?' I cajoled.

'Well, it was durin' the war,' Erchy began. 'There must have been a big wreck some place out here an' there was lots of stuff came ashore one night. The Rudha folks got word of it an' they was all waitin' to grab it. Trunks packed with money, folks say there was, an' they hid it all away. There was plenty of corpses too, scattered all over the shore, so when they'd taken as much stuff as they wanted for themselves the Rudha people told us an' then they told the pollis. Ach, it was a dirty trick,' said Erchy with disgust creeping into his tones. 'Anyway, the pollis didn't come out straight away so as soon as it got dark me an' Tearlach went over there to see would we find anythin'. All we found was bolls of flour, plenty of them, and corpses, dozens of them too, all over the shore. An' the moon was shinin' on them so that they gleamed an' the tide was washin' round some of them makin' their limbs move so that you'd think they were tryin' to get up. God! We got that scared we just lifted a boll of flour on to each other's back an' we ran home with it as fast as we could go. Indeed I don't believe we stopped for breath until we got to within sight of Anna's house, an' we never went back there again neither.'

The path to Rudha was four miles of narrow sheep track along the shoulder of the hill, below which the land slid steeply to the jagged rocks of the shore. Even in broad daylight the uninitiated take one look and either turn back or tackle it quakingly on all fours.

'An' then the pollis came,' continued Erchy, 'an' they took away the corpses but they left the bolls of flour. The rest of the folks here just went then and helped themselves.' He sighed. 'That's all Bruach ever got out of it—a few bolls of flour, except for Tearlach's dog that got a good feed off one of the legs of the corpses,' he added reflectively.

I put on the tablecloth. 'Your mother will be giving you up for lost,' I reminded him.

'Aye,' he said, without much interest and, still havering in the doorway, he turned to look out into the night. 'Did Hector tell you he has a buyer for his boat?' he asked over his shoulder.

'No,' I replied with some surprise. 'Has he really? Who?'

'Ach, some fellow down Oban way, I believe,' answered Erchy, turning round again and leaning against the edge of the door. 'He's asked me will I sail it down there with him on Friday if the weather stays this way.'

'And are you going?'

'Aye. I might just as well. Seein' we're goin' we're takin' Johnny Comic to the dentist. The poor man's near crazy with the toothache.'

'That's rather a job to tackle, isn't it?' I asked. 'Johnny's never been away from here before, has he?'

'No, an' he's that scared of comin' with us I believe we'll have to put a rope on him first.'

'You'll never get him into the dentist's chair,' I warned, suspecting that Johnny's one idea would be to play hide-and-seek with his companions until they could delay their return no longer.

'Ach, Tom-Tom's comin' to hold him,' said Erchy. 'An' there'll be the two of us if we're needed.' I stared at him in surprise. 'Aye, you can look like that,' he told me, 'but gentle as Johnny is he's a strong man when it comes to strugglin' an' he'll struggle well enough if he thinks he's goin' to have somethin' done to him.' He edged half of himself outside the door and started to pull it to behind him. 'Is there anythin' you'll be wantin' us to bring back for you? We'll likely be doin' some shoppin'.'

There was always at the back of my mind a list of things which I intended to ask people to get for me should there be some prospect of their visiting the mainland. Now, confronted with Erchy's sudden question, I could recall only the relatively unimportant fact that when the previous autumn I had wanted to make use of some small green tomatoes—the grudging produce of a dozen troublesomely acquired and carefully nurtured plants—I had no vinegar to make them into chutney. It was no use even asking the grocer if he stocked it, for the crofters though lavish in their use of salt were as yet not conditioned to, or perhaps aware of, the other condiments. One never saw a bottle of sauce on a Bruach table.

'Would you bring me a bottle of vinegar?' I asked, still vainly struggling to recall some more needful item on my mental list.

'Vinegar?' repeated Erchy in a puzzled voice, and then, as enlightenment slowly dawned, he went on: 'Aye, I mind now what you mean. Vinegar's the stuff they put on chips in Glasgow, isn't it?'

He was outside the door by now and letting in a gently chill breeze that was bringing up the gooseflesh on my sun-tanned arms.

'Hector's supposed to be bringin' back a few chickens for Morag,' he informed me. 'You'll not be wantin' any yourself, will you?'

'That is a good idea,' I responded with enthusiasm. The only chickens one could get in Bruach were the hardy progeny of the inveterate fowls that scratched around every house and cornstack, flaunting their mongrel feathers with the aplomb of peasants attired in their national costume. I had once tried to get pure-bred chickens sent up to me simply to find out if they laid better, but the length of the train journey coupled with the capriciousness of the local carrier had ensured that none of the chickens had survived. I asked Erchy to bring me a dozen day-old chicks—Black Leghorns if they were available.

'I'll do that,' he promised, and then perhaps because he remembered he was going in a leaky old boat on an unpredictable sea, or perhaps because he recalled a previous experience of high life in Oban, he added a cautionary, 'If the Lord spares me.' He sounded a trifle embarrassed. 'I'm away. Good night,' he called, and shut the door.

'Good night." I rejoined and sat down at last to eat my supper.

There was a clouding over of the sky in the late afternoon of the following day and the next morning the sun, which had shone unrestrainedly for so long, only cocked a sleepy eye before retiring beneath a canopy of grey cloud. It looked as if the spell of fine weather was coming to an end. Friday morning dawned wet and windy with the sea flouncing angrily against the rocks and with grey sweeps of rain being hurried across the bay. When I went up to the village shop to buy paraffin I espied Erchy, Hector and Tom-Tom leaning in various attitudes of disconsolation against the gable of the latter's house. All were gazing with equal gloom at *Wayfarer* who was plunging and rearing at her mooring.

'You're not going off today, then?' I observed.

'No damty fear,' replied Erchy. 'That sea is goin' to get bigger before it gets smaller.'

'There's some big enough lumps out there already,' said Tom-Tom. 'I don't fancy it myself.'

'We're safer where we are,' agreed Hector with glum acceptance of the situation.

'Well, here's one who's mighty pleased we're not settin' foot on the sea,' said Erchy with a wink and a nod towards a hunched figure which squatted miserably beside him. 'Is that not so, Johnny?' he shouted, and in answer the figure raised a face that would normally be described as being of 'ashen hue'. However, when one has become a burner of peat as opposed to coal it is a description one can no longer use, for 'ashen' would imply the complexion of a Red Indian.

'Poor Johnny Comic,' I said. 'Is his toothache still as bad as ever?'

'No,' denied Erchy. 'You cannot have toothache an' be scared out of your life at the same time. You can only feel one or the other.'

We were joined by Morag who was also on her way to get paraffin.

'So my brave boys has decided it's too rough for them,' she said by way of greeting, and the men turned away, discomfited by the derision in her voice. I picked up my can and moved away. Morag walked alongside me, a smug grin on her face.

'It doesn't look very nice out there, does it?' I remarked.

'Ach,' she said disdainfully. 'They're not much of sailors nowadays. I've seen my father go out in seas three times as big as I'm seein' out there an' their boats not half the size either.' She turned and gestured towards the bay. 'I've known myself be out in more sea than there is now.'

'Morag,' I demanded. 'Have you ever been out in a sea big enough to frighten you?'

'Only once that I mind,' she confessed with a slight grimace of shame.

'Was it very rough then?'

'Ach, it was all yon big green beasts that you can see through. Comin' straight at us they was till you thought with every one of them that the boat would never ride the next. My father made me lie down under one of the thwarts so that I wouldn't get thrown out.' She sighed. 'Aye, we were caught badly that day an' I believe I was as frightened as I've ever been. Mind you,' she added hastily, 'frightened though I was, I was never what you'd call inebriated with fear.' She chuckled. 'I was younger then, though, an' I daresay I hadn't as much sense as I have now.'

With our cans filled with paraffin we started off for home again, stopping frequently for me to change my can from one aching arm to the other. Morag, who was carrying twice the amount of paraffin, did not put hers down for an instant and only watched my struggles with a tolerant smile. Hector and Erchy were still propping up the end of Tom-Tom's house but by this time they had been joined by Old Murdoch and Yawn who had doubtless come to offer cautionary advice although at this moment they were engaged in conversation with a young girl who stood, slim and straight, between the two bent old men, like an 'I' in parenthesis.

'Yon's the lassie that's been stayin' with Mary Ann over the last few days,' said Morag in a low voice. 'You'll have seen her likely?'

'Only in the distance,' I admitted.

'She was askin' Hector last night would she get back to the mainland with him today an' he had to promise her he'd take her.'

'I should jolly well think he would have promised,' I muttered as we drew closer. She was quite the most beautiful creature I had ever seen, with huge brown, lustrous eyes, dark curly hair, exquisitely fine bones and a skin of such goldenness that it looked on this dull day as though it was exuding sunshine. Even I felt momentarily stunned by her appearance. What she did to men I could only guess.

'But, Hector,' she was saying with wheedling fretfulness as we approached, 'you promised you'd take me. I would have gone on the bus this morning and caught the ferry if I'd thought your boat wouldn't be going. I've simply got to be back in the office in London on Monday morning or I'll get the sack.'

Hector only hunched his shoulders harder against the wall and looked sulky.

'Ach, you'll not get the sack,' consoled Erchy. 'Tell them you got held up by the storm an' it'll be all right.'

'I can't tell them that,' she retorted.

'Why not?' demanded Erchy.

'They wouldn't understand.'

Erchy grunted his scepticism.

'It'll maybe get a bit calmer by this evening yet,' Yawn prophesied, and the girl who, despite the fact that her teeth were chattering, still managed to look ravishing, brightened up visibly.

'Will you take me across this evening then, if it gets calm?' she coaxed, with a look at the men that should have sent them hurrying to launch any number of boats.

'Ach, no,' said the usually impressionable Hector, shuffling uncomfortably. 'Tse tide will be all wrong by tsis evenin' for gettin' the dinghy off the shore.'

The girl's expression as she turned to me was a mixture of chagrin and disbelief.

'Please,' she begged. 'They don't seem to understand

how terribly important it is for me to get back. It's a new job I've landed—quite a good one and I wasn't really due a holiday yet but they kindly let me have these few days. Will you try to explain to Hector for me?'

I shook my head, understanding her frustration but by now almost as out of touch with her world as were the rest of the group.

'Well,' said Erchy with decision. 'You say you cannot get back to London by Monday morning unless you leave here tonight. An' you cannot leave here tonight so you cannot do anythin' else but wait.'

'They'll not take it so badly if you just explain to them that it was the storm that kept you back,' soothed Yawn. 'An' the tide,' he added as an afterthought.

The lassie drooped with dejection. 'I've told you,' she reiterated. 'You can't explain to people in London about things like that. They'll never believe it,' she finished with a grim smile.

Yawn was visibly staggered. 'They wouldn't believe you?' he demanded.

The lassie shook her head.

'Well, lassie,' he advised her with great gravity, 'I'm tellin' you, you'd best never go back at all to a place like that. If they don' understand about storms and tides and things they must be a lot of savages just.'

'Miss Peckwitt and Morag! Is it yourselves?' Tom-Tom's wife appeared round the corner of the house. 'Come away in now and take a fly cuppie with me. I have it ready.'

We followed her inside, and the men, anxious to evade the lassie's continued importunings, lumbered after us.

'Honest to God,' grumbled Erchy, as he seated himself on the bench. 'Some people thinks it's us that makes the weather.'

'Aye, an' tse tides,' rejoined Hector. 'Some of tsese folks tsat come in my boat, tsey say to me, "Can I leave tsis picnic basket," or sometsing like tsat. "Will it be all right here on tse shore till we get back?" And tsen when I tell tsem no, tsey must take it up on tse rocks out of tse tide's way, tsey tsink I'm not bein' nice to tsem.' He shook his head sadly.

'It just seems as though they don't understand about the tides,' said Erchy wonderingly.

'They know the theory but not the practice,' I said. 'They learn about tides ebbing and flowing but they're not taught that this means the water is always moving up to or away from the actual bit of beach they're sitting on.'

Hector gazed at me with serious surprise. 'Tsey shouldn't need to be taught tsings as simple as tsat,' he assured me. 'Tsey didn't teach ourselves.'

As I drank my tea I studied Hector covertly, for I had just witnessed him do a thing which I had always thought him incapable of doing and that was to remain impervious to the charms of a young and beautiful girl. I was curious to know the reason for it.

'Isn't that lassie a beauty?' I hazarded.

'Eh?' said Erchy stupidly.

Tom-Tom's wife thought for a moment. 'I don't believe

she's so bad at that,' she conceded.

Hector looked up from his tea. 'Ach, what good is she when she's tsat tsin you could use her for darnin' a sock,' he observed with a grin, and looked at the other men for confirmation.

Tom-Tom's wife, who had once been described to me as being 'not fat but needin' an awful lot of room when she sat down', chuckled appreciatively. I stared at Hector. He had never before struck me as being particularly figure conscious when selecting his female companions. What then, I wondered, was there about this girl that he should find her so uninteresting?

'She tsinks too much of herself, tsat one,' he explained, as though I had asked the question aloud. 'I was down on tse shore tse usser day,' he went on, 'and she comes along. She was after lifting tsese coloured stones from tse beach to take back wiss her and when she sees me she drops tse bag and she says: "Oh, Hector, I'm so glad I've met a big, strong man to carry my stones for me. Tsey're awful heavy," she says.'

'An' did you carry them for her?' questioned Morag with a wink at me.

'Indeed I did not,' responded Hector. 'I told her if she'd managed to carry tsem tsat far she must be stronger tsan she tsought she was, so she'd best carry tsem tse rest of tse way.' His blue eyes were impish as he looked at each of us in turn, expecting our approval. 'You know she was tsat vexed wiss me she hardly spoke to me all tse way home.'

'I don't understand it,' I said. 'I would have expected

every man in the place to be following her. I'll bet she's used to plenty of attention in England.'

'Well, she'll no' get much of it here,' Erchy stated flatly.

'And yet she's what I'd describe as a real beauty queen,' I mused.

'I'm no' seein' it tsen,' scoffed Hector. He took a noisy gulp of tea. 'I believe she's only one of tsese foreigners anyway and she's queer.' He frowned down at his cup. 'I wouldn't want to take anytsin' to do wiss her anyway, for no religion has she at all but a bit of wood or stone.'

All weekend the clouds raced greyly above a shaggy sea but on Monday night there seemed to be a promise of calm in the night sky and on Tuesday morning I woke without the sound of rain on my windows or the wind bullying the roof. In Bruach one's life was so inextricably bound up with the weather that one got into the habit of waking with an ear cocked for the sound of wind much as, after an illness, one wakes to the expectation of pain. If there was no noise of storm in a morning one waited tensely, hesitating to believe the miracle and then when one had accepted it one would throw off the bedclothes and hasten to get started on the labours of a busy day.

By the time I returned from milking Bonny *Wayfarer* had left her moorings and was already a dark speck on the horizon. Within a few days NellyElly, the postmistress, had received a telephone message from Erchy saying that Johnny had been taken to the dentist and that Hector had bought himself a new boat in which they now proposed to sail back. She reported that he had sounded quite sober. For two or three days there was no word from the men and so it was assumed that they were already on their way. Those of us who had binoculars went frequently to lean our elbows on the stone dykes and stare out to sea, hoping to be the first to pick up a sight of the mariners and send the word round the village. For easily diverted people like myself it was an excuse to scan the outlying islands, trying to identify their varied peaks or, nearer home, to focus the glasses on the constant industry of the sea birds; on cormorants fishing greedily; on busy, bobbing guillemots and on the swift dipping flight of terns over the sea, contrasting their activity with the motionlessness of a stately heron standing beside the mouth of the burn, and then, ruefully, with my own idleness.

But a week went by without any sign of the boat and when on the following Tuesday morning the mist rolled in from the sea, thick as a sponge, and hid everything beyond the boundaries of the crofts, we knew we could not expect to see them for some time. I wondered if Morag and Behag, Hector's wife, were worrying about the lack of news and felt I ought to go along and ceilidh with them for the evening. When I pushed open the door of Morag's cottage there came the sound of many voices.

'Come away in,' called Morag happily. 'Come in and see the rascals.'

Erchy, Tom-Tom and Hector, their faces shining in the lamplight, were seated at the table enjoying a meal of salt herring and potatoes. There was a partly full bottle of whisky on the table and a couple of empties down in the hearth. The men looked mightily pleased with themselves.

'How on earth did you get home on a day like this?' I asked them.

'We came in Hector's new boat. How would you think?' replied Erchy waggishly.

'Did you have a compass?'

'We did not, then. What would we be wantin' with one of them things, anyway?'

'But isn't the mist as thick on the water as it is here on the land?' I wanted to know.

'Twice as thick,' pronounced Erchy. 'We kept catchin' the boat right bangs. Hector said they was only hard pieces of water but I believe we hit every rock between here and Oban.' He broke open a large floury-looking potato and stuffed almost the whole of it into his mouth. He turned to Hector. 'She's a good strong boat you have there,' he told him, with an accompanying slap on the back. 'She must be or she'd be in bits by now.'

Hector smiled bashfully at the herring he was holding in his two hands.

'Seriously,' I taxed them. 'How did you manage to navigate if you didn't have a compass?'

'Ach, well, we was just goin' round in circles to begin wiss,' explained Hector. 'Every time tse mist lifted a bit we saw tse same bit of coast one side of us or tse usser. We was keepin' close in, you see, trying would we creep round tse shore.'

'Aye,' Erchy took up the tale, 'and then I remembered

how my father had told me about bein' caught in the mist on the sea once. He tore up a newspaper he had in the boat and scattered bits of it on the water as he went so he'd know if he was goin' in circles. We did the same just. We did that all the way and it got us home here, safe as hell.'

It sounded like a story I had heard before and ought to have more sense than to believe. 'Is that true?' I asked doubtfully.

'As true as I'm here,' asserted Erchy, and to this day I do not know whether he was pulling my leg.

'You didn't tell us yet how Johnny got on at the dentist's with his teeths,' said Behag quietly from the bench where she was sitting patiently with three alert kittens and the irrepressible Fiona all helping her to knit a fair-isle sweater.

The three men gave a concerted hoot of laughter. 'You should have been there to see it,' Erchy said. 'Johnny went and sat in the chair like a lamb and we didn't think he was goin' to give any trouble at all, but the dentist took one look at him an' decided he'd best give him gas. That was all right and he took the tooth out after a bit of a struggle, but then he must have taken the gag out too soon or somethin'. Anyway, he had his thumb right inside Johnny's mouth when suddenly Johnny's teeths clamps down on it. My, you should have heard that dentist shoutin'. He started swearin' at his assistant an' the assistant swore back and told him what a fool he was to his face. He got his thumb out at last, but by God! he was in a state, I can tell you. Then Johnny comes to, an' feelin' his bad tooth's out an' not hurtin' him any more, his face lights up and he jumps up from the chair an' rushes at the dentist shoutin' "By God! By God!"' Here they were all overcome with laughter. 'The poor wee dentist mannie didn't know Johnny only wanted to shake hands with him and thank him for gettin' his sore tooth sorted for him,' resumed Erchy. 'He was terrified! He thought Johnny was after him to do him some hurt an' there he was runnin' round and round the surgery holding his thumb with Johnny chasin' after him still shoutin' "By God! By God!" like he always does when he's excited. "Get him out of here!" the dentist yells at us. Screamin' he was too. "Get the bugger out of here before he kills me." Well, me and Tom-Tom manages to get hold of Johnny and drag him out. Poor man was that puzzled about it all so I went back an' told the dentist that Johnny had meant him no harm, it was only that he was wantin' to thank him.' Erchy disgorged a mouthful of herring bones on to his plate. 'Ach, but he wouldn't listen to me. "Don't you ever let him inside here again," says he. "I might never be able to pull another tooth the way my hand is now."'

'Poor man,' ejaculated Morag half-heartedly, but I did not know to whom she was referring.

'Did you bring any chickens?' I asked after a pause.

'Aye, so we did.'

'Black Leghorns?'

'Aye.'

'Black Leghorns!' shrilled Morag with an acerbity that was mellowed by the tot of whisky she had just swallowed. 'Drunk Leghorns more likely!'

'Drunk?' I echoed with a smile.

'Aye, drunk,' affirmed Morag, lifting the lids of two cardboard boxes near the fire.

'Aye,' Erchy started to explain. 'You see we got them three days ago when we first thought we was startin' back. Well, then we met up with some lads we knew and we had a good drink with them so we didn't wake up in time to get goin' the next day. The lads came again the next night so we stayed and had another good drink. We'd forgotten about the chickens, you see.'

'I didn't forget tsem,' repudiated Hector who was beginning to doze in his chair. 'I gave tsem a wee taste of oatmeal I scraped up from tse linings of my pockets.'

Morag snorted. 'For all the good that would be to them you might just as well have left it there,' she told him.

'Well, as I was sayin',' resumed Erchy, 'we didn't think about the chickens until sometime last evenin' when Hector says all of a sudden: "My God! What about them chickens?" So we fetched them out of the wheelhouse where they'd been all the time and we had a look at them. They didn't look bad and they was makin' plenty of noise but they was huddled together just as though they was feelin' the cold.'

'Sure they was feelin' the cold,' interpolated Morag. 'The poor wee creatures.'

'What did you do then?' I encouraged.

'We didn't know what to do,' said Erchy. 'We had no coal on the boat to put on a fire and no other way of warmin' them, until Hector said we should try would we warm them with our own breath. So that's what we did. We took it in turns just to go and give them a good breathin' on every now and then. Is that not the way of it, Hector?'

Hector again roused himself to confirm his own brilliance.

'But how did they get drunk?' I persisted.

'Ach, well you know how it is, Miss Peckwitt. These lads we met, they came down again and they'd brought a few bottles with them, so we started drinkin' again. We minded not to forget the chickens though an' we kept openin' the lids of their boxes and givin' them a good warmin' with our breaths. I remember thinkin' one time that they looked to be gettin' sleepy. Their eyes was closin' and they started staggerin' and lyin' down with their legs stretched out. I thought they must be dyin' all right but Hector said no, they was lyin' down because they were goin' to sleep as they should.' He laughed. 'Ach, I think we was both pretty drunk then.'

'I would have expected Johnny Comic to have mothered them like a hen,' I said.

'He didn't know a thing about them,' said Erchy. 'As soon as he stepped back on the boat he rolled himself in his oilskins and lay in the bunk there and he stirred only to eat one of the hard-boiled eggs Kirsty had given him when he came away. Honest, she gave him three dozen of them!'

'They're no' lyin' down any more,' said Morag, taking another peep into the boxes. 'They're no' very strong but they're up on their feets.'

'Am I not after tellin' you it was just drunk they was. Drunk on too much whisky fumes,' said Tom-Tom who, since finishing his meal, had sat smiling foolishly at the coloured plates on the dresser as though he was watching a chorus of dancers.

'The poor wee things,' said Morag again. 'Day-old chicks and so drunk I'm thinkin' they'll not reach a day older before they're dead.'

But she was wrong. 'The poor wee things' not only survived but thrived exceedingly well. They seemed to be immune from all the maladies that can affect young chickens and not even Morag had ever known such wonderful layers.

III. *Tourists*

NELLYELLY, HER SON DUNCAN, Erchy and Hector were all looking slightly baffled when I called at the Post Office.

'It's a glorious day,' I greeted them enthusiastically, and though they were emphatic in their agreement that it was indeed a glorious day and went on politely to acclaim the benefits such weather would bring in the way of increased crops and increased tourism there was an air of preoccupation about the four of them. I wondered if it had anything to do with the folder NellyElly had in front of her on the counter.

'Ask Miss Peckwitt what she thinks about it,' suggested Erchy.

'Yes, well,' said NellyElly hastily. 'I was about to do that just.'

I looked from one to the other.

'It's like this,' the postmistress began to explain. 'We've just had a telegram through for one of the young men that's campin' down by the burn there—yon dark boy who wears the thick glasses and chews bubbles when he talks, you mind?'

I nodded, puzzling as to what the difficulty might be.

'Well,' went on NellyElly, with a trace of reticence, 'it seems it's his twenty-first birthday and the sender's paid for one of those special birthday greetings forms for him and I haven't one left in the place.'

'And now,' Duncan continued for her, 'if we give it to him on a plain form just an' he finds out it was a fancy form that was paid for, somebody might be after puttin' in a complaint.'

'What sort of forms have you, then?' I asked, trying to be helpful.

'Just these,' said NellyElly, handing me two forms, one of which was decorated with wedding bells while the other was gay with storks.

'One's for weddings and the other's supposed to be for the birth of a baby,' she explained superfluously. 'Those are all I have except for the plain forms.'

'I'm sayin' she should send him tse one with tse birds on,' suggested Hector. 'Tse poor man might get a bit of a fright if he gets a wedding telegram right in tse middle of his holidays.'

'It depends on the message, I should think,' I said.

'It says just "Congratulations on your twenty-first",' NellyElly read out obligingly.

'In that case I should think he'd get much more of a fright if he got a telegram with storks on it,' I said with a levity that was not particularly well received.

'Which sort of tsings is storks?' demanded Hector.

'Those birds,' I told him, indicating the telegram form. 'They're the ones that are supposed to bring the babies.'

'Aye?' His expression was one of polite disbelief and I realized that of course Bruach had never indulged in such pleasant euphemisms.

'Well, will one of us go down an' ask the man which form he'd like best?' suggested Erchy.

'Ach, no.' She seemed doubtful. 'Maybe if Duncan took it down on a wedding form and explained to the fellow that it's all we have just at the moment, likely he'd take it all right?'

'Likely he would,' we comforted, and so she wrote out the message and gave it to Duncan. Erchy and Hector accompanied him so as to witness any possible reactions.

I gave my letters to NellyElly and she tried the date-stamp experimentally on her bare arm. 'Ach!' she ejaculated. 'Fiona was in last night and was playin' with my stamp.' She adjusted it and again applied it to her arm before stamping it on to the envelopes. 'There now,' she said, dropping the letters into the box.

She came round from behind the counter to close and bolt the door of the Post Office behind me. It was only three in the afternoon but she was going to hoe her potato-patch beside the road and from there she could see any potential customers. She was not to be left long undisturbed, for Bruach already had its first quota of tourists and I had left the Post Office only about a hundred yards behind me when I met a pair of sun-scorched and midge-bitten campers sauntering along the road, who demanded a little resentfully to know where the Post Office had hidden itself and if, when they found it, they could buy stamps there. They implied both by their tone and their remarks that they had found Bruach a little unaccommodating so far. I directed them on their way but their resentment had kindled a response in me, not against Bruach or the Bruachites but against the tourists themselves, for they were coming now in their coachloads and carloads, robbing the village of its privacy and awakening the hibernating avarice of the crofters.

The moment the first tourists arrived (always pronounced 'towrists' in Bruach) the crofters began to look more alert. Except for the old die-hards like Yawn, who would have nothing to do with tourists and only gave them a 'withdraw the hem of his garment look' when they ventured near him, they thoroughly enjoyed the colour and the air of prosperity the presence of the visitors imparted to the village. Soon notices began to appear outside croft houses adjoining the roadside, proclaiming that they were 'Tearooms' or offering 'Bed and Breakfast', and of these there were more than enough to cater for the number of people who came. Some drew more custom than others, perhaps because of their position, perhaps because of the fare they offered, but it was comforting to see how little rivalry there was between them. Admittedly, Hamish, having been dissatisfied one season with the amount of trade his wife's tearoom had attracted, had tried to increase it the following season by the added lure of a 'toilet', and with this intention he had erected a notice-board in his front garden. Painstakingly, because he was crippled with rheumatics, he had painted the word on it in large white letters, but unfortunately spelling was not Hamish's strong point and he was soon having to endure much mockery from his neighbours for having left out the 'i' so that the notice stated somewhat confusingly 'Tolet'. In an attempt to rectify his mistake he had hastily inserted an 'i' in the appropriate position but the letters were already so cramped that it merely looked like an emphatic full stop separating the words 'To' and 'let'. That at any rate is how the tourists interpreted it and throughout that season Hamish and his family were pestered by people anxious to rent their thatched cottage, until Hamish, almost beside himself with vexation, had resolved to clarify the position beyond doubt in time for the next season. This he had done by simply adding the letters 'W.C.' above the 'To.let' already on the board. I do not know if it brought increased custom to his tearoom but I do know that whenever I passed by Hamish's cottage there were groups of puzzled tourists studying the sign and debating among themselves as to its meaning.

However, on Sundays, despite the presence of tourists, Bruach reverted to its normal piety. Sheets put out to bleach were taken in if they were dry, or, if they were still wet, rolled up so that the sun should not be employed to whiten them. In some houses male guests might be asked if they would mind shaving on the Saturday night because the landlady could not allow the use of a razor on the Sabbath, and always, last thing on Saturday night, the 'Tearoom' and 'Bed and Breakfast' notices were draped over with sacking, though with such artful nonchalance that the words were never completely obscured.

'He Breeah!'

I paused and turned round in the direction of the hail to see Janet talking to Dugald who was at work in his potatoes. She waved an indication that she was about to join me and I sat down on the grass verge of the road while I waited for her. The hot sun was burning through my dress and the parched grass was warm and brittle against my bare legs. The breeze was soft as thistledown and spiced with lark song, while out in the hay a school of porpoises plunged and tumbled with consummate grace. Close inshore a trio of shark fins cut lazily through the water. We were well into the second week of long days that began with the sun poking its fingers into one's eyes in a morning and ended, after molten sunset, in a calm and soothing twilight that all too soon merged into another dawn. The cuckoos, who all day answered their own echoes until it seemed they would drive themselves and everyone else crazy, only decelerated their pace during the night—they did not cease altogether.

'Ach, mo ghaoil,' puffed Janet as she struggled up the steep bank. 'Whenever are we goin' to see the last of this fine weather?'

'Are you tired of it?' I asked her.

'Indeed, I'm no tired of the weather but I'm tired of

bein' short of water,' she grumbled. 'My brother's complainin' he has time for nothing else all day but going back and forwards to the well for me.'

It was always the same when we got a nice spell in Bruach. We could not really enjoy it after the first few days because by then we had begun to fret about our water supply.

'I have that many sheets to wash,' resumed Janet, 'an' there's more visitors comin' tonight. An' even when I get the water the well is that low it looks like I'm washin' the sheets in strong tea.' She swung her sack of bread over from one shoulder to the other. 'Indeed, that woman I have stayin' with me just now came out to speak to me while I was doin' my washin' yesterday an' you should have seen the look she gave to my water.' Janet chuckled tranquilly.

'Is that the woman from Manchester you were telling me about?' I enquired.

'It is so, mo ghaoil, an' that's what I was wantin' to ask you about. She's sayin' she feels it that strange here an' she's just longin' to meet another Englishwoman. I was wondering would you come over and have a wee crack with her this evenin' and cheer her up a bitty?'

'I can't come now,' I apologized, for in Bruach 'afternoon' receives no recognition. It is morning until about two o'clock and then it becomes 'evening'. 'I've promised to take Fiona for a picnic and I don't suppose I shall feel much like going anywhere but to my bed when I get back from that.'

'No, indeed,' agreed Janet understandingly, for Hector and Behag's small daughter was a notoriously intractable child.

'Will I tell her you'll come tomorrow, then?' Janet pleaded, and when I agreed she grasped my hand thankfully. 'She'll be fine an' pleased when she hears it, for she's like as if she thinks she's among a lot of savages.' Janet's laughter bubbled again. 'Indeed, d'you know she asked me the other day if there was coal mines beyond the hills because they reminded her so much of the "slack heaps" I think she called them she's after seein' in England.'

'Why ever did she come here?' I asked, feeling vaguely affronted.

'Ach, well, I believe her husband used to come to these parts an' he was always after praisin' it up to her so when she lost him she thought she'd best come here an' see what he liked so much.'

'What a good thing she didn't come with him and spoil it for him,' I said.

'That's just what I was sayin' there myself to Dugald. The woman's a right misery to herself because she can't see a single factory chimney no matter how hard she looks.'

The sandwiches and cake for our picnic were already prepared and I had only to pack them into a bag and then collect Fiona. She was bobbing impatiently in the doorway and as soon as she detected me she ran towards me, shouting all the way.

'Dugald's just away and he says you're to get rhubarb tonight on your way back.' She tugged at my hand, pulling me round so that we faced in the opposite direction to which I had planned. 'We're goin' this way,' she announced.

'No, we're going this way,' I told her firmly. The trouble

with Fiona was that she was so used to getting her own way she was completely deaf to correction. She continued to pull me in the direction she wanted to go but on this occasion I had resolved that I must be equally firm.

'I am going this way, Fiona, and if you want to go the other way you may. We'll share out the food now.' It was a risk because she was quite capable of agreeing to go off by herself and I should then have had to trail surreptitiously in her wake to make sure she came to no harm. Her sudden capitulation appeared to stagger her as much as it did myself for she was too speechless to issue a single command while we plodded over the brittle dry moors and picked our way across the beds of dried-out burns.

'Why did you no' want to go the other way?' she demanded when she had regained her complacency, and while we helped each other to descend a narrow path that led to a beach which Fiona had never visited before and which I loved for its seclusion I explained to her why I had chosen to come this way. It was really to avoid Bonny, for when I had first bought her and put her out on the hill with the rest of the village cattle she had been friendless and alone for a time and so whenever she saw me she had got into the habit of following me. I had made the mistake then of packing a 'wee potach' for her along with my own picnic lunch and had then had to endure her standing over me ecstatically chewing a juicy green cud from which webs of saliva drifted all over my own food. The next time she had spied the lunch bag on my shoulder she had grown impatient for me to open it and had insisted on escorting me so very closely that when I had come to the stepping-stones of a burn and had stood poised hesitantly in the middle she had urged me on so eagerly with her horns in my back that I and the lunch bag had emerged in a wet and sorry state. Her devotion to me was touching and because of it I did not try too much to discourage her until she had progressed from being merely accepted by the other cattle to become the acknowledged leader of the younger set. Then I had to find a different location for my alfresco meals. It was one thing to take one's own cow for a picnic. It was quite another to take thirty or forty other cows, each one of them curious to discover what it was in my lunch bag that was so attractive to their leader.

Fiona stared at me expressionlessly as I talked and when I had finished she asserted flatly, 'See that boat out there,' as though she had not listened to a word I said. She was looking out across the listless water through which a ringnetter was tearing its way with emphatic urgency.

'She has plenty fish,' she added with adult self-assurance.

'How do you know she has fish, clever puss?' I teased.

'Because she has the gulls with her,' replied Fiona through tightened lips. She did not call me a silly old cailleach as she would have had I been her mother or aunt, but her tone was unmistakable. I stared out at the ringnetter. There was a trail of fuzzy smoke from her galley chimney and in it the gulls whirled and eddied with the sun glancing off their wing tips so that it looked as if the boat had thrown over herself a gauzy, sequin-studded scarf.

I suggested beachcombing, a pastime which the child revelled in and which I found at least as pleasurable as at one time I would have found a shopping spree in town. It added to one's feeling of self-sufficiency and independence to gather driftwood for one's fire and in addition there was always the exciting prospect of stumbling upon a really worthwhile find. Our progress was slow for Fiona demanded my attention for even her most trivial finds and her chatter was incessant. However at last we found for her a brightly coloured ball and then almost simultaneously a coir door-mat and a perfectly good plastic pail. She was momentarily overawed by her good fortune until she recollected our picnic.

'When will we take our tea?' she asked with only partially concealed impatience.

I waited only to pick up my own finds—a brass port-hole with glass intact that I thought would improve my front door and two aluminium net floats which Erchy would halve for me to provide four typically Bruach feeding bowls.

'We'll have it now if you like,' I told her. We sat down cautiously on the sunbaked rocks with our bare feet in a warm, tide-washed pool that was floored with pounded shells and studded with sea-anemones, and when we had eaten we played at sailing Fiona's ball until the sun had moved off the cliff-screened shore and the midges began to work up to their evening appetites. We climbed up to the open moors again, our feet disturbing hundreds of heather moths which fluttered up in front of us like petals chased by a gamin breeze. The sun was still shining with evening-tempered brilliance; the sheep were just beginning

to rouse themselves from their siesta; a lamb bleated for its
mother and was answered by the frustrated mew of a buz-
zard planing overhead. Fiona's fat little legs plodded stur-
dily beside my own but she had gone very quiet and I
suspected that she was tired. I hoped she had forgotten
Dugald's message and planned to deposit her back with her
mother and aunt before I went to collect the promised rhubarb. But of course she had remembered and of course she
insisted on accompanying me, although it would add another mile to our walk. I gave in without argument.

Dugald's croft ran alongside the road and was recognizable by a large notice stating that it was a 'Car Park,
price 1/-', a notice which had been erected originally more
as a piece of bluff than anything else but which was now
appreciably augmenting Dugald's pension. It had been at a
ceilidh one evening that Dugald had been complaining bitterly that the tourists' cars were ruining his hay and someone had then suggested that the best way to stop the cars
from parking on his croft was to make them pay for the
privilege. Dugald had thought it an excellent idea and had
immediately erected the notice, but to his bewilderment
instead of continuing along the road where there was ample
free parking space the foolish drivers still came and parked
on his croft. For some days Dugald had tried to look as
though neither the house nor the croft belonged to him
when he saw honest drivers looking for someone to pay
their shillings to, but when, from the concealment of his
byre, he had watched them go to the cottage and hand the
parking fee to his wife, Dugald had been so shaken that, as

he put it, 'I didn't know what to say to myself.' When he saw how the shillings mounted up he realized that he was on to a good thing and now Dugald was soon out of the house and waiting for his fee whenever a car so much as put a wheel on his croft. Except of course on Sunday.

Dugald was changing the calves' tethers when we saw him and made our presence known. He shouted that his wife was away on the bus but that there was rhubarb for me at the house if I would get it. Fiona and I opened the door of the porch and took the large bundle of rhubarb that would not only provide me with puddings for several days but would also be enough for a couple of jars of jam. I went over to thank Dugald and as he had finished the tethering he was ready and willing to spare a few minutes for conversation.

'She was sayin' you'd get more if you're wantin' it,' he told me. (Crofters when speaking English never seem to know how to refer to their wives, for in Gaelic it is 'cailleach' which is literally 'old woman' and they realize that this is not quite acceptable to polite English people.)

'If she has plenty I'd like some more,' I told him. 'I could use it for making wine.'

'Aye, she has that much of it we could do with throwin' some of it in the sea,' he told me. 'You'd best come up after you've taken your dinner tomorrow and get some more.'

'Not tomorrow I can't,' I replied. 'I've promised to go and talk to that woman Janet has staying with her. Janet says she's lonely and miserable.'

'Is that the one they had out in the boat today to show her the scenery and she just sat with her head bent over her knittin' all the way so she didn't see a thing?'

'It sounds like her,' I agreed.

'Ach, well, likely she will be miserable,' said Dugald. 'She's from Manchester, isn't she?' he added, as though that explained everything.

'How's the parking business going these days?' I asked him with a grin, to which he responded with an oblique smile.

'Ach, no' bad, no' bad,' he said with studied offhandedness. 'Though there's some of these drivers that comes an' all they give me instead of a shillin' is a mouthful of argument.'

'I was hearing great praise of you from a motorist only the other day, anyway,' I told him.

'Which was that?' he demanded with sudden suspicion.

So I told him of a driver I had been talking to who had parked on his croft the previous Sunday, and who had gone to the cottage to pay his parking fee only to be confronted by Dugald who had refused the shilling with stubborn piety. The man had been so impressed that as soon as he knew I was not a Gael he had burst out with the story. He had never believed, he had told me, that he would actually meet a man so implacably devout as to forgo his rightful dues just because it was the Sabbath.

'Ach, that cheat,' said Dugald, when I had finished. 'He was English too, I mind.'

'Cheat?' I repeated.

'Aye, cheat, I said. He parked his car here all day from early in the mornin' till late at night an' not so much as a sixpence did I get out of it.'

'But he told me he had pressed you to take the money but you refused.'

'So I did,' said Dugald virtuously. 'I explained to him once or twice that I couldn't take the money from him because it was the Sabbath.'

'Well, in that case how can you say now that he was a cheat?' I demanded with a touch of amusement.

'Could he no' have left it on the windowsill for me?' replied Dugald with shattering apostasy. 'It would still have been there for me in the mornin'.'

Both Fiona and the midges were becoming increasingly persistent in their demands that we should move and, slapping at our bitten limbs, we fled down the road to Morag's cottage where Hector and Erchy were enjoying a strupak. This season the boats had swapped partners and now the two friends were happily running the *Ealasaid*, Hector's new boat, together. Their greeting to me sounded slightly ironic.

'You don't sound too happy,' I told them. 'Haven't you had as good a day as you'd expected?'

'Good enough,' replied Hector. 'But we're only just back from our last trip.'

'That was a late one,' I said, taking the cup of tea Morag was holding towards me.

'Aye, and we didn't get paid for it either,' said Erchy.

I looked at them searchingly. An unrewarding boat trip so often meant that there had been a climbing accident. 'Ach, but these English are mean,' said Erchy with a slow shake of his head, and Morag and Behag shot placatory glances in my direction. I laughed.

'Goodness!' I said. 'I seem to be hearing nothing but stories of English meanness today. What has been happening to you two?'

'It was a fellow we took on the boat this mornin' that went climbin' in the hills. When we went back for him this evenin' we found him sittin' on the shore near crazy. He told us he'd come to a very narrow ridge and the only way he could cross it was on his hands and knees. When he was halfway across his wallet slipped out of his pocket an fell down the steepest part. He said it had fifty pounds in it.'

'Didn't he go after it?' I asked.

'Ach, he was in no state to go after it," retorted Erchy. 'He was shakin' all over like a leaf when we found him an' that must have been two hours after.'

'What happened then?' I prompted.

'Well, we had our people waitin' on the shore to go back an' we couldn't just leave them there so we brought them back an' him along with them. Then we went back to see would we find the man's wallet.'

'Could he describe where he'd lost it?'

'Aye, indeed we knew fine where it was likely, but that didn't mean it was any easier to get. Hector near broke his back tryin' would he reach it an' there was that many stones fallin' down we were both of us in fear for our lives.'

'But you got it?'

'Aye, we got it at last an' when we came ashore here there was the man waitin' on us. We waved it at him so he'd know to stop worryin' an he came runnin' down the shore fast as a deer an' grabbed it out of my hand. Me an'

Hector, we waited while he opened it, thinkin' maybe we'd get a bit of a reward or maybe the hire of the boat just for goin' back for it, but all that man did was to take out the notes there in front of us an' count them. When he'd finished he gave us a nice smile. "Fifty pounds," he says to us. "All intact, gentlemen. Thank you very much," an' away up the road he goes without leavin' us as much as the price of a dram between us for our trouble.'

Hector shook his head. 'It was him countin' tse money tsat made me feel so bad,' he said sadly. 'Just as tsough we might have been after stealin' some of it.'

'Aye,' said Erchy, 'but that's the English for you.'

'Maybe he was that glad to see his wallet he just didn't think to give you anythin' at the time,' interceded Behag.

'Ach, the man must have had no brains at all if he wouldn't think of a thing like that,' said Erchy.

'He had brains all right,' asserted Hector. 'The folks tsat came on tse boat with him was tellin' me he was a Doctor of Divinity.'

'Ach, but you don't need brains to be one of those sorts of doctors,' said Morag knowledgeably. 'You see, you don't need to have any practice.'

The following afternoon I put on my latest summer dress (made from material purchased through a mail-order catalogue), picked a bunch of flowers from my garden and set off for Janet's house prepared to do my bit towards entertaining the difficult visitor. Janet came out to the gate to meet me and exclaimed delightedly at the sight of the flowers.

'She's havin' a wee bitty lie down on the sofa,' she told me. 'Wait now till I get a wee somethin' to put the flowers in an' then I'll tell her you're here.' She found an empty jug and drained the cold contents of a teapot into it.

'Good heavens!' I ejaculated. 'Is water as short as that with you?'

'It's gettin' that way,' she confessed. 'My brother's sayin' we'll need to drink whisky instead of tea if the well gets much lower. It takes that long to fill a pail now he's there all day.' She twitched the flowers into position as an impatient dressmaker twitches at an ill-fitting dress, and then put the jug on the table. 'Beautiful just,' she murmured. 'Come away in now an' we'll see is she awake.'

In the other room a torpid figure, its face covered by a newspaper, lay along the couch beneath a window that framed a picture of islands dozing tranquilly in a wideawake sea that the sun was sowing with stars; of hills that were dreamily remote behind a tremulous haze of heat; of a sky that was blue and white as a child's chalk drawing, scuffed by a woolly sleeve. The figure pulled itself to a sitting position.

'Ee, luv,' she said in a voice that was so coarse it made me feel dishevelled, 'whatever made you come to live in a god-forsaken place like this after England?'

She said, 'I think I'd go daft if I had to live here among a lot of strangers.'

She said, 'You know, luv, just seein' you come through that door and knowin' you've lived near Manchester, it's just like a breath of fresh air to me.'

Erchy said the next day when I was down on the shore

giving my dinghy a coat of paint: 'Here, I'll take back what I said about the English yesterday. I'm thinkin' some of them aren't so bad after all.'

'Oh,' I said, with only conventional curiosity, 'and what has changed your mind?'

'Yon woman that's come to stay this week.'

'Not,' I interrupted him, 'not surely the woman from Manchester?'

'No, but the one who's come to stay with Kirsty. Now she's what I call a nice woman. We took her for a trip in the boat this mornin' an she gave us a good tip on top of her fare.'

'Good,' I said. 'I'm glad we're not all to be condemned.'

'Ach, some are all right, I suppose,' acknowledged Erchy grudgingly.

Hector sprackled up to us. 'Tsat Englishwoman's wantin' a boat for tomorrow to take her to see tse caves just by herself,' he said. 'She says she'll hire tse whole boat.'

Erchy looked startled. 'Did you tell her how much it will cost her?' he asked Hector.

'Aye, I did so, but she just said "money's no option".' Hector rubbed the back of his neck. 'I've never heard anybody say tsat before in my life.'

'She's away with Ruari this evening in his boat,' I observed.

'Aye,' agreed Erchy. 'She told us she likes goin' about on the water so she's goin' to share out her trips between the different boats. That's partly what I meant when I said she's a nice woman,' he explained as he moved away.

The children came out of school in a rush and with barefooted nimbleness picked their chattering way along the road. The day quietened as the boats disgorged their last passengers and the noise of labouring coaches receded into the distance.

'Did you get a tip from yon woman that's stayin' with Kirsty?' Erchy called out to deaf Ruari as they were making fast their dinghies for the night.

'Aye, I did that,' responded Ruari with all the power of his stentorian voice. 'I got a whole crown from the bitch.'

'I do envy you being able to understand the Gaelic,' said the 'nice woman', who had paused to watch me as I put the last touches to my dinghy and who was screened by a rock from the sight of the two men, 'it's such a quaint-sounding language.'

I do not know if Ruari's voice had diffused the sound so much that she had not been able to distinguish the words or whether she had chosen this way of saving all our faces but when Ruari and Erchy came abreast of the dinghy and saw her still there she talked them easily out of their confusion and was still talking to them with great animation as she walked between them to the brae.

'Here,' said Erchy anxiously when I next met him. 'D'you think that woman heard what Ruari said last night? Honest, I thought she was a mile away or I would never have asked the man.'

'I don't think she heard,' I assured him.

'I wouldn't like to think she was offended,' he said, 'she's such a nice woman.'

Whether or not she had heard the remark it seemed to have given no offence, for she continued to patronize the boats and to tip generously. In return the boatmen greeted her warmly whenever she appeared and even bestowed on her the accolade of an invitation to go with them on the free trips they sometimes ran in an evening for their friends. She confided to me one day that she had never before in her life had such a wonderful holiday and her praise for the boatmen was unstinted. When at length her holiday came to an end she astounded them by presenting each of them with a bottle of whisky.

'Didn't I tell you she was a nice woman?' demanded Erchy when I congratulated him on the gift. He took the bottle out of his pocket and gazed at it with great reverence. Then his voice changed and he seemed to recoil from the shock of his own words. 'A nice woman, did I say she was?' he questioned, with another fond glance at the bottle. 'No, indeed, but I should have said she was a nice *lady*!'

IV. *The Election*

'Did you get a bit of venison from the Laird last week?' enquired Morag as we were returning from milking our cows one frost-still autumn morning.

'No,' I replied. 'Did you?'

'Surely we did,' she informed me. 'I thought everybody got a bit.' We parted company for a moment, she to pick her way round one side of a patch of bog while I went round the other. 'It makes a laugh the way he gives us a wee bitty venison as if he's givin' us a five-pound note,' she continued as our paths rejoined. '"I hope you'll find this nice and tasty, Morag," says he, thinkin' likely that it's a rare treat for us.' She giggled. 'An' so it would be I doubt if all the venison we got was when he has a mind to give it to us.' Her face wrinkled in an allusive grin. 'Indeed, many's the whole stag of his I've eaten if he did but know it,' she confessed shamelessly.

'Why the generosity?' I wondered.

'Likely it's the Election,' explained Morag with her usual astuteness. 'Maybe you didn't get a piece because he thinks you're a Socialist,' she added.

Until the announcement of the forthcoming General Election politics had rarely cropped up as a subject for conversation at the ceilidhs and when it had it had always been in a bantering and inconclusive way. Even after the announcement there was no vestige of what could be termed 'election fever' in the village. Old men ventured to make sketchy references to such subjects as tariffs and free trade, and Murdoch, the village's only militant Tory, was once or twice reduced to stuttering inarticulateness by the tauntings of a couple of the younger blades with professed leanings towards Socialism, but invariably the skirmishes ended if not in complete agreement then in good-humoured laughter. The Bruachites did not have much time for subjects from which they could not extract some fun one way or another.

As the Election drew nearer it became apparent that Bruach was going to vote almost exclusively Tory, for in contrast to their normally uncompromising individualism the Bruachites displayed a curious desire for conformity in superficialities. How often have I heard the wily tinkers successfully inducing people to buy a child's dress or a woman's overall simply by exaggerating the number of identical ones they had already sold in the village. And when the biannual request for donations to the church came round the sum shown against the first name on the list was always dittoed for all the rest of the names. Similarly, when the hospital appealed for eggs everyone was careful to give the same number as his neighbour. Except for one uncomfortable occasion when the Grazings Officer sent round a list asking for the dates of bull servings and got it back with so many dittoes that a hundred and twenty seven cows were shown as having been served by the same bull on the same day, the duplication appeared to be perfectly acceptable to everyone.

However, when it came to deciding at the ceilidhs what advantages they wished the Government to provide the Bruachites reverted to their usual policy of amiable disagreement.

'What we're needin' before anythin' is a pier,' declaimed deaf Ruari with a combative look in the direction of any dissenters.

'We've been promised a pier by every government since I was a lad,' returned Yawn easily. 'But I didn't see it yet.'

'It'll come. It'll come yet,' soothed old Murdoch amidst grunts of disbelief.

'No, but what we're needin' first is a good road, the way we won't have to get the heavy things on the steamer and then have to carry them all the way up the brae,' argued Big John between gulps of baking-soda from a tin on the mantelpiece.

'Aye,' seconded the irascible Donald, who as the owner of a tiny motor boat chose to believe there existed between him and the steamship company as much rivalry as exists between competitors for the Blue Riband. 'We could finish then with Messrs. David MacBrayne and Company, nineteen twenty-eight limited,' he exulted with his accustomed preciosity. During the summer Donald ran trips in his boat to local places of interest. The steamer did likewise but with far more comfort and a great deal less hazard—hence the antagonism.

'If we got the watter we could ask them for a lavatory for the public,' piped up Sheena, who was unfortunate enough to live in a cottage which adjoined the road near a spot much favoured in the season for disgorging busloads of tourists. Glassy eyed with discomfort after the rough ride and too urbanized to trust themselves to the privacy of the moors, the tourists' first thought was to prospect for some shed they might break into and foul. 'I canna' gather but a handful of peats from the shed without there's dung or piss on it,' Sheena complained.

'Aye, that's the way of it,' confirmed Morag, with a nod.

'If it's a lavatory we're wantin' then it's in the burial ground we should be gettin' one first,' asserted Erchy. 'Never mind the tourists.'

'A laventory? In the burial ground?' expostulated old Murdoch. 'Whatever for, man?'

'They have them in other places,' Erchy told him. 'Two of them sometimes: one for men and one for women.'

'God knows what for, then,' said Murdoch, shaking his head bewilderedly. 'Surely they're not believin' the dead get up and walk?'

'It's for the folks who go to the funerals,' shouted Erchy

above the tittering, and Murdoch's brow immediately cleared. 'You know how it is when you're at a funeral,' Erchy went on, 'you always feel you can't wait to drop your pants. If it's outside the gate you go then it's likely one of the women will get a hold of you so you can't get away. If you try inside the damty place is so full of graves somebody starts shoutin' at you for defilin' his grandfather or somebody.'

It struck me that in contrast to the demands of the more cosseted townsman they seemed to want very little from their government. There was no appeal voiced for factories to provide regular employment, no general desire for larger crofts, no agitation for higher pensions. Perhaps it was because in the cosy atmosphere of the ceilidhs the Bruachites were entirely honest with themselves. They did not want the discipline of industry in addition to that already imposed on them by storms and tides. Their crofts were as large as they could comfortably manage without mechanical aids. On the matter of pensions they kept wisely silent for in Bruach there was no pride about receiving Public Assistance. Rather was it a source of rivalry to see who could wheedle the most out of the authorities and at times one got the distinct impression that the recipients regarded the payments as in the nature of prize money for the best storyteller. Their avarice was both shocking and amusing and I well remember an occasion when, as I was waiting to board the train at the mainland station en route for a visit to Glasgow, I had suddenly been hailed by a lady whom I knew had been drawing Public Assistance for years.

She was dressed neatly in black with touches of that sparkling whiteness I believe only Highland rainwater can impart to a fabric, and had I not known her I should have
thought from her dignified bearing and the quiet authoritativeness of her manner that she was at least a duchess.
We greeted each other cordially and agreed it would be
nice to travel together.

'There are some empty compartments down there,' I
said, inclining my head towards the rear of the train.

My companion gazed at me with sorrow and surprise.
'Oh, but those are all second-class compartments down
there,' she told me. 'You'll surely not be travelling second
class, will you, Miss Peckwitt?'

'Why, yes,' I replied. 'Aren't you?'

'Oh, no, mo ghaoil,' she responded without a trace of
embarrassment. 'I always think one meets such common
people travelling second class.' She scanned the train and
then turned to me again. 'Will you not change your ticket?'
she begged with affected concern, for she had just spotted
a more desirable acquaintance who was beckoning to her
from the genteel end of the train.

'No,' I said firmly. She shook her head in mock reproof
but her mouth relaxed into a lenient smile as we parted,
she to step regally into a first-class compartment while I
wilted into a second.

I recall too the time when there came to reside temporarily in Bruach an old lady whom the Bruachites invariably referred to as 'yon rich old fool'. However when the
'rich old fool' had been in the village for some months she

revealed, with a discernible pride in her achievement, that she too had joined the ranks of those receiving Public Assistance. The crofters were scandalized and her revelation was tossed from person to person along with comments that were as disparagingly hostile as if she had gatecrashed an exclusive club. Of course they never for an instant believed that she was not still a rich old woman; but I never again heard anyone refer to her as a fool!

Though I once heard of a crofter who was too proud to accept Public Assistance or to allow his wife to accept it whilst he was alive, the story was accepted by the rest of the Bruachites with the same mocking half belief as they accepted such tales as of the man who had grown a third leg and of a child who had been buried out on the unhallowed moor because it was born with two heads.

It was not long before we began to hear of various election meetings being held in neighbouring villages more accessible from the mainland than Bruach itself, and if there was a pub and the owner of the bus could be persuaded to run a cheap trip then there was always a fair contingent from Bruach willing to listen courteously to anyone who might care to practise his rhetoric upon them. They would titter at all his witticisms, they would murmur appreciatively at the aspersions cast by party on party, but they rarely heckled and it was quite impossible for a stranger to guess in which direction their loyalties lay.

Inevitably the Election began to impinge on our lives. The postman arrived later and later. 'These bloody election letters,' he explained. 'Honest, they keep me back worse than the pools.' Eventually our ballot papers arrived.

'Here,' said the postman conspiratorially as he followed his bulging mailbag through the open kitchen door. 'Just you take these from me and put them under the kettle.'

'What are they?' I asked him, immediately suspicious.

'Ballot papers,' he replied. 'Put them under the kettle, I'm tellin' you.'

'I daren't!' I told him.

'Ach, they're only for my cousin Tearlaich,' he explained, 'and the bugger will only be after spoilin' them by votin' Socialist.' He held the envelope towards me, but I drew back shaking my head, and when he moved as though towards the stove I stopped him firmly. It was then that I caught the glint of laughter in his eyes so that I was not deceived by the air of disappointment he assumed as he slipped the envelope back into his bag.

'What would you have done if I'd snatched those papers out of your hand and put them under the kettle?' I taxed him.

He met my enquiry with a broad, delighted grin. 'Damned if I know,' he admitted unregenerately.

A brief spell of crisp bright days ended with bitingly cold winds that flung great sloppy raindrops at the frost-skinned earth. On the moors the bracken, so stately in its youth, so wanton in maturity, now lay brown and sad among the rocky outcrops while in the boglands the peat hags filled with dark water. It was while we were enduring this sort of weather that there came word that a representative of the Socialist candidate would be holding a meeting in the village schoolroom the following evening. Bruach was a little staggered.

'We must be gettin' well known,' said Yawn facetiously. 'Why else would they be botherin' to come out here when they didn't before?'

'Didn't come before?' ejaculated Morag. 'Indeed they did so.'

'I never mind them comin',' maintained Yawn.

'Aye, well they did so,' reiterated Morag. 'Murdoch will tell you, will you not, Murdoch?'

Murdoch, thus appealed to, looked thoughtful for a moment and then said with great confidence, 'Aye, of course I mind fine them comin' here.' He turned to Morag. 'Was that no' the year we salted the herrin' before we cut the corn?' he asked her.

'It was indeed,' confirmed Morag. 'An' it was good herrin'.'

'Aye, aye, it was good herrin',' agreed Murdoch, removing his pipe. There was a recognizable moment of nostalgia while Murdoch's spittle sizzled on the glowing peat.

'Will you be goin' to listen to the mannie tomorrow if you're spared?' Morag asked me as we were saying good night.

'I suppose so,' I replied. 'We should go and hear what he has to say.'

'Well,' said Morag, 'it would no' be very nice for him if people didn't go and take a look at him after him goin' to the trouble to come out here for us.'

So the following evening, braving the inexorable rain,

I went along to the schoolroom which, by the time I arrived, was already nearly three-quarters full of chattering, chaffing adults interspersed by a sprinkling of sober, wide-eyed children. The mingled smells of damp peaty tweeds, stale dogs, dungy boots and pipe smoke, all shot through with the sharp, clean smell of wet oilskins, met me as I stood by the door looking for a suitable seat. Morag caught my eye and beckoned me over to a spare desk between herself and Behag and even as I compressed myself into it there was a chorus of warning coughs from the porch and a purposeful middle-aged man attended by two smug confederates made his way to the teacher's desk. A courteous hush fell as he was introduced to us by one of his aides.

'Here, but I know that man well,' confided Morag, who, I believe, attended all such gatherings as much to exercise her quite remarkable memory for faces as for any other reason.

'Who will he be, then?' whispered Behag with a sudden spurt of interest.

'Why, but that Willy John. His father used to live up at . . .' She and Behag went off into a mixture of reminiscent Gaelic.

'What does he work at now, then?' enquired Behag, obviously far more curious about the man's pedigree than in what he had to say.

'Ach, well, I believe he was a cobbler one time, but then he went away to the war,' Morag recalled. 'He was wounded in the hand I was after hearin' and he couldn't carry on with his cobblin'.'

'Poor soul,' said Behag. 'What does he do now?'

'Ach, they sent him off to one of these places where they rehalibutate people and now he's a fish buyer,' Morag told her. 'They're sayin' he's doin' well at it.'

'Whist you, Morag,' some of the people behind enjoined us after they were satisfied that Morag had completed her identification. The representative was standing up and we composed ourselves to listen to his address, but from the moment he opened his mouth we felt ourselves stiffening as if we were being coerced into a conflict, bewildered as to its cause and with the certainty of our own defeat. His words smote us; the breaths he occasionally paused to exhale seemed to sear us, and when the meeting came to an end we found ourselves feeling curiously sorry for him for having given us such a bad time—and wishing he would soon go so that we would have time to feel sorry for ourselves. Nevertheless we sat and clapped him dutifully and with confident smiles he left us.

'My, my' exclaimed Morag as we emerged from the schoolroom, feeling bruised with politics and cramped and chilled after our damp contortions in the tiny desks, 'that man's voice was that rough I believe I could have struck a match on it.'

The following morning I awoke with all the signs of a vicious head cold and although I heard that the Liberal candidate was sending a representative to the school that evening I put out my light early to discourage ceilidhers and went to bed. My cold was little better the next day, so that I missed also the representative of the Tory candidate, who, not to be outdone, had arranged to hold a meeting that evening. By the evening of the third day I was feeling thoroughly wretched, my cold obstinately refusing to yield to my usual remedy ('It came itself, it can go away itself'), and I had resolved that as soon as my chores were finished I would take myself off to bed with a couple of aspirins, a large glass of hot milk and some extra blankets and try to sweat it out of my system. It was therefore with some dismay that I found Ishbel, the elderly spinster half-sister of Katy, the shepherd's wife, waiting for me when I returned to the cottage, but I managed to sniffle a tepid welcome. She seemed satisfied and sat down on the edge of a chair with her usual nervous hesitancy that reminded me of a fledgling just before it launches itself from the nest.

'I mustn't stay,' she demurred.

'Of course you must.' I tried to infuse some decision into my voice.

'No, but I heard you had taken the cold so I thought I'd best come along and see if you needed help.'

I thanked her warmly but assured her that it was really only the discomfort of the cold that worried me.

'It's that Socialist fellow gave it to you,' she declared with more asperity than I had ever heard in her voice. 'I knew the moment I heard him speak he'd brought the cold to us.'

'Possibly,' I agreed. In Bruach once the holiday season was over colds were infrequent and when one ravaged the village it could invariably be traced to someone who had 'gone to the mainland for a cold' or to some infected visitor.

'I'd never vote for him after that,' threatened Ishbel, whose childish rule of exacting indiscriminate retribution, however trivial the incident, was something of a joke in the village; she had once slipped on a piece of orange rind and broken her arm so she had never eaten an orange since.

'Are you takin' anythin' for your cold?' she asked, reverting to her normal timidity.

'Just hot milk and aspirins,' I told her.

She delved into her bag and brought out a half bottle of whisky which was at least two-thirds full. 'Now, I want you to take this,' she adjured me. 'A good glass of this tonight before you go to your bed an' it'll see your cold away by the mornin'.'

I was overwhelmed by her kindness. 'Thank you very much indeed,' I said, 'but really—'

'No, but I want you to have it,' she interrupted me. 'I've had this stuff in the house since I took the cold myself near thirteen years ago now. I didn't take the cold again to this day so I've not had but the one dose of it.' She put the bottle down on the table. 'Whisky keeps all right though it's been opened,' she assured me.

'Of course,' I murmured and thanked her again. 'But,' I objected, holding up the bottle to the light, 'I shan't want all this. I'll just take out a dram and you take the rest back with you.'

'No, indeed I will not.' She stood up, clutching her bag as if to prevent any attempt to foist the bottle back on her. 'I'll away now and let you get to your bed but you'll see and take a good dram of it before you go?'

I promised.

The following morning I was still snuffling when Erchy called to give me a bundle of dried carragheen and also the startling news that the Socialist candidate was proposing to address a meeting at eight o'clock in the Bruach schoolroom.

'The man himself,' Erchy emphasized. 'You'd best come an' listen to him.'

'Not unless my cold clears up a bit during the day,' I replied.

'Ach, but you shouldn't have a cold today,' he remonstrated. 'I was after hearin' you got some whisky from Ishbel last night to take for it. You couldn't have taken a right dram if you still have a cold. The whisky would have killed it.'

'I didn't take much of a dram,' I confessed with an involuntary shudder. 'And neither would you if you'd been in my place.'

'Why not?' enquired Erchy.

'The bottle had been opened thirteen years ago,' I began, but he cut me short.

'It doesn't matter. Whisky keeps all right,' he assured me with an authoritativeness that I felt sure could only have been based on hearsay.

'Oh, yes,' I agreed. 'I've no doubt whisky keeps all right but it also takes up the smell of mothballs.' I grimaced. 'It was the foulest-tasting mess I've ever tried to swallow. She must have had the bottle packed round with camphor for all of thirteen years.' I picked up the bottle and held it towards him. 'Here, smell it yourself.'

Erchy took a cautious sniff and then groaned. 'The daft old cailleach,' he commented.

But apparently one small mouthful of camphorated whisky had its effect on my cold for by evening my head had improved wonderfully. When eight o'clock came I wandered down to the school. There was not an empty desk to be had and I had to insert myself into the knot of men who were packed around the door. The candidate had already begun speaking, wooing the crofters with glib promises of prosperity but completely alienating them, if only he knew it, by predicting the setting up of rural industries so that they could supplement their croft incomes without recourse to Public Assistance. Nevertheless, he left happily assured of their support.

'I canna' understand that man. They tell me he has letters after his name so he must be clever. You wouldn't think he'd want to go spoilin' himself with Parliament,' opined Morag, who seemed to be under the impression that the nomination of a candidate was arrived at in much the same way as was the selection of the village 'bull tender' and that the field of choice was similarly limited to those with no aptitude for more exacting tasks.

In the wake of the Socialist candidate came the Liberal, who also held a well-attended meeting in the schoolroom. I had a date with my wireless set that evening so I did not hear his address but I have no doubt that he too was completely convinced that he had won the confidence of the Bruachites. I asked Erchy when I next saw him how the meeting had gone.

'Ach, that man!' replied Erchy scornfully. 'He didn't seem to know what to say to us at all. Indeed I don't believe he was sure if he was goin' to vote Liberal himself.'

It seemed that the Conservative candidate did not consider the votes of Bruach's small population vital enough to warrant a personal appearance and Morag and old Murdoch among others had to endure some innuendoes from those who feigned rebellion simply to take a rise out of the older folk. Then, on the afternoon preceding polling day, when I was mixing the evening mash for the hens, Morag came scuttling into my kitchen with the air of apologetic excitement that always assailed her when she had urgent news to impart.

'The Conservative candidate is here,' she burst out enthusiastically, 'an' he has a loud halo.' She had predicted all along that he would come. 'Come away outside and listen to him,' she insisted. I put down the bowl and followed her out into the garden where the booming voices of the first loudspeaker van to visit Bruach could be heard wafting an invitation to everyone to be present at eight o'clock at the school that evening to meet the candidate in person.

'Well!' I ejaculated. 'So you were right. But imagine Bruach having a loudspeaker van. They must think we're important.'

'Aye,' agreed Morag, 'but I wonder at them goin' to all that expense when our own Ruari could have shouted it just as well without any batteries to work him.'

Whether it was the 'loud halo' or the reputed wealth and social position of the candidate that animated the village I do not know but by a quarter to eight (unprecedented punctuality for the Bruachites) the school classroom was packed as full as only Gaels can pack themselves, and people overflowed into the porch and even, though it was a chilly night, out into the playground. Everyone appeared to be present from the oldest grandfather to the youngest child and the air shimmered with expectancy.

'I see even Angus's father has managed to get here,' I observed to Morag, who had pushed her way to my side. Angus's father was an obstinate old man who spent the periods of relative mobility between crippling attacks of rheumatism sitting on the grass verge beside the road and would not be cajoled or coerced away from it.

'Aye, well, he's no' so bad when he's on the flat bit of road,' Morag told me. 'It's when he comes to the ingredients he canna' manage.'

The candidate was very late, but there was no audible discontent, and when he did arrive the company clapped him with a vigour that was strangely out of keeping with their normal show of reserve. As he rose to address us an almost servile silence descended and everyone listened with apparent avidity, though many eyes wandered frequently from his rather long hair to the casual dandiness of his clothes, only to be arrested again and again by his expansive gestures. At the end of his speech one or two people ventured to ask questions, but he answered them with nimble assurance and when the meeting officially came to an end he remained behind, still affable and approachable, ready to discuss the trials of a crofting life.

'My,' observed Erchy reverently at the ceilidh which followed, 'that's a nice fellow if only he'd get his hair cut.'

There was exultation among the old folk. 'That's our man,' they all agreed. 'You mind what he promised us about the pier?'

'What does it matter what he promised you?' young Hamish demanded. 'Once they get into Parliament they don't bother what they said to folks before.'

'Maybe so, maybe so,' admitted Murdoch, hurrying to prevent Yawn from voicing scepticism.

'An' supposin' he does get us a pier from the House of Commons then it only needs the House of Lords to throw it out and we're back worse off than when we started.' Hamish was becoming eloquent in his dissatisfaction. 'The first thing the Socialists will do is to get rid of the House of Lords,' he promised. 'There's no damty good at all in that place.'

'Here, no,' Murdoch rebuked him.

'Indeed, yes,' responded Hamish, with increasing fervour. 'What good does it do, anyway? Tell me that now.'

Murdoch pondered for a moment or two, rolling his unlit pipe in the palm of his hand. 'Well,' he began, 'what I say is, the House of Lords is just a big ceilidh house; sometimes they have a wee bit talk over things, sometimes maybe a wee song and maybe a dram at times or a wee strupak, just like ourselves here.'

'An' what the hell use is that?' Hamish's voice was shrill with derision.

'Ach, well,' said Murdoch. 'I'm thinkin' many's the time

there's been troubles in this place but when they've been talked over at a couple of ceilidhs likely they've soon been sorted.' It might be as well to explain here that in Bruach everything is 'sorted'. You go to the dentist to get your teeth 'sorted'. Similarly you go to the doctor to get your ailments 'sorted'. And if the engine of your boat gives trouble you send for someone to come and 'sort' it.

Hamish gave an ironic grunt and moved towards the door. 'The trouble with you lot is you won't give a man your vote unless he has plenty of money,' he flung at them as a final taunt.

Had he stayed he would have found me in wholehearted agreement with him, for I am convinced the crofters prefer their M.P. to be wealthy, their attitude seeming to imply that whereas there is a possibility of a rich man being satisfied with what he already has, a poor man is inevitably a greedy one.

Polling morning brought a perceptible rise in temperature with a sun-tinted wind chasing a genial haze of rain through the glen. Voting was scheduled to start at nine o'clock in the morning but not until all the croft work was finished and the bus driver had taken his tea did the crofters trouble to get themselves ready. The polling station was in a neighbouring village at a tiny disused school and the bus was ready to take the voters at sixpence per head, but I chose to walk, for the uncertain day had matured into a perfect autumn evening with the hills hardly more than a murmur of golden serenity behind shrouds of gauzy mist. My path lay along the coast and below me the bay spread out like a broad blue apron, ruched with dark rocks and dotted with resting gulls like white French knots. Earlier in the year the evening would have been marred by swarms of rapacious midges so that one would have needed to smother oneself in protective lotion or envelop one's face in fine veiling, but now the midges had disappeared and one could swing along heedlessly and rejoice in the beauty that was everywhere.

Angus, short, wizened and briskly genial, called to me as he was shifting the tether of a cow to a fresh patch of grass. He was wearing polished shoes instead of his usual gumboots.

'Are you away to the votin'?' he asked.

'Yes,' I replied. 'Are you and Jeannie going?'

'Ach, Jeannie'll no' be comin', she's near dead with the cold,' he answered. 'But I'm goin' along myself.'

'What about your father? Is he going to triumph over his rheumatics to vote?'

'Ach, my father could get over his rheumatics right enough,' said Angus, 'but he says he's no' puttin' in his teeths just to go and put a wee cross on a piece of paper.'

The bus, packed with passengers who waved with decorous condescension, passed me, but it had to stop so often along the road to pick up hesitant or late voters that it arrived at the polling station only a few minutes before I did. The crofters, self-conscious in their best clothes, were just alighting and there were shouts and imprecations as ecstatic sheepdogs, who had chased after the bus all the way from the village, greeted their owners and tried to insist on following them into the school.

The schoolroom was very small and was tastefully decorated with jars of white, strongly scented flowers which I had never seen growing anywhere but in the most sheltered corner of the burial ground. The two bored voting officers sat cuddled together at the teacher's inadequate desk on which cups of tea, a plate of buttered scones and a dish of jam reposed hospitably between the box containing our voting slips and the official black ballot box. The polling arrangements would have made wonderful propaganda for an enemy. To mark our cards we were in turn directed to a cupboard which stood against the wall at right angles to the window. The cupboard was just large enough for a small person to get inside but if one closed the door it was too dark to see what one was doing. If one left the door open then everything one did was easily visible to the prospective or spent voters who loitered with carefully assumed indifference outside the window.

When I came outside again Big John, who stood six foot three and was of pugilistic build and yet the mildest of men, was leaning nonchalantly on the sill watching a confused Sarah peering in her shortsighted way at the voting slip which she held in her two hands. Sarah frowned; she pulled at her lips. John gave a commentary on her predicament and there was a stir of laughter. We all knew Sarah couldn't read anyway. At last she held her card up to the window and her mouth framed a question. Big John pointed. Sarah nodded and smiled with relief and bent over her card, the pencil grasped in her shaky fingers. John rapped peremptorily on the window and Sarah's perturbed head bobbed up. John gesticulated. Again Sarah nodded and bent over her paper. John relapsed into nonchalance.

'Silly old cailleach nearly voted for the wrong fellow,' he told us.

V. *Tinkers' Wedding*

THE FOLLOWING SUMMER was drearily wet and was succeeded by an autumn that was distinguishable only by the shorter hours of daylight and by the waning appetites of the midges. For those of us who had not been hardy enough to ignore the constant rain (the less resilient under-sixties, it seemed) croft work dragged on interminably. Most of my potatoes were as yet undug. My peat shed was only a third full, the rest of the peats being still in their stacks on the moors waiting either for me to carry them home, creelfull by slow and heavy creelfull, which I had been endeavouring to do all summer, or for the track to dry out sufficiently for them to be loaded on to a lorry. I even had hay still out on the croft in sad, dark cocks which were so soaked with rain that they were able to resist the teasings of the strengthening winds.

'I doubt a right gale will come before long an' put your hay away for you, but not where you're wantin' it,' predicted Yawn smugly as he passed the croft where I was working. I answered him with a feeble grin, recalling how savagely a gale the previous autumn had dealt with almost the whole of Donald Beag's carefully made stacks of hay. Into a night of mist and calm the gale had come suddenly, announcing its arrival by a staccato rattle of the new tiles of my cottage roof. By the time I had shut the bedroom window and buttressed the front door with a shaft of wood it was already thumping against the windows, blasting noisily into the chimneys and hissing venom at the leafless elder bushes. For two hours it had blown turbulently and then, with only two or three faint whispers of apology for the commotion it had caused, it had gone, leaving the unsettled night to be soothed by the dolorous tick of the rain. Daylight had revealed that all that was left of Donald's hay harvest were the wisps and shreds that were caught in the wire netting of neighbouring hen-runs. The Bruachites secretly gloated. Donald was easily the hardest working man in the village and the fact that he made his croft pay caused some resentment. They had lost no time in seeking him out to witness his dismay whilst at the same time offering perfidious commiseration.

'What happened to all your hay, Donald?' they asked him innocently, and Donald, who was perfectly aware of their feelings, only laughed and, waving a facetious hand towards one of the outlying islands, replied, 'It's all in Sandy's barn over there, I reckon.'

The end of October drew near and then it was Halloween. Stags were roaring in the hills. The rams were already
among the sheep. The Department of Agriculture bull had
been caught and sent to his winter home. Through wind
and rain I worked desperately at my potatoes so as to have
them all lifted before November came. Admittedly, unlike
my neighbours, it was not so much the disgrace of having
croft work still unfinished on the first of November that
spurred me on. It was the knowledge that, though a date
well into the middle of November was always decreed by
the local Grazings Officer as being that on which all cattle
could be brought in from the moors and allowed to roam
the crofts, as soon as a few of the more idle or less tolerant
inhabitants had themselves fenced their haystacks and put
away their spades for the winter, moor gates were liable to
be left insecurely latched so as to swing open at the nosing
of a curious cow, or after dark they would be deliberately
opened so that one was apt to wake up to find cattle driving
their horns deep into one's carefully stacked hay or fighting
one another over one's precious potato patch. Resolutely
ignoring my stiffening back I plunged the fork into the
earth, lifting the roots and picking off the potatoes one by
one, examining each for signs of blight before throwing it
into the pail which in turn had to be carried to the shed
where they were to be stored. The floor of the shed was
already covered with dry peat dust and on top of this had
gone a layer of heather and dry bracken. On to this cosy
bed went the potatoes, to be covered, when the lifting was
finished, with more heather and bracken and then with a

layer of old sacks. I was assured my potatoes would now be safe from everything except pilfering mice.

Mercifully, all my hay was in the barn and by tea-time on Halloween I had reached the final row of potatoes, digging in a deepening twilight that was aided by a mist of fine rain and enclosed in a silence that was pierced only by the occasional lament of a homeward-bound gull, the scrape of my fork into the stony ground and the thud of potatoes into the pail. The musty autumn smell of the moors was strong in my nostrils, reminding me of how the village children would even now be excitedly rummaging into musty sheds and spidery lofts for even mustier clothes in which to dress themselves for their evening ploys. Their simple Halloween 'false-faces', made from a sheet of cardboard bent round the face and tied with string at the back of the head, would in snatched and secret moments already have been chalked or painted with fearsome white fangs, staring multi-coloured eyes and then liberally trimmed with fleece from the spring shearings, before being hidden away to await the great night. I recollected that some parents had expressed doubt as to whether the children would have the courage to go out this year because of the reported presence of a 'white beast' or as some described it 'a wee white man' in the hazel copse which filled a cleft of the moor between my own croft and the skirts of the hills. In the autumn the copse was a favourite nutting place not only for the children when they came home from school but for any adults who had time to pick or teeth to crack the nuts, but this season, after the first pickers had returned visibly shaken to tell their stories, the copse had been completely neglected.

'D'ye believe in the wee folk yourself, Miss Peckwitt?' Old Anna had asked, and because I refused to be drawn she went on, 'Are ye no' afraid, livin' all by yourself down there?'

I had told her that I was not afraid but now, straightening my aching back for a moment and looking across to the copse looming spectrally through the drifting mist, I wondered if it was still the truth. No, I was not afraid, but there is no denying that in the twilight of a still evening the moors, wild and deserted yet full of whispers, can have a disquieting effect. They seemed to breathe their mystery down my neck as I picked up a full pail of potatoes and carried it up the croft to the shed, refusing to let myself hurry yet conscious that my torso seemed to be well ahead of my legs. I emptied the pail and resolutely went back to my lonely digging.

'I see you're busy.' I jumped so much that I stuck a tine of the fork through the toe of my new gumboots and turning round saw the postman grinning at me from under his peaked cap. He was wearing uniform but there was a rifle under his arm and the mailbag was full of dead rabbits.

'I'm about finished,' I told him, indicating the half dozen or so sticks of withered haulm still unlifted.

'They're no' bad,' he complimented me after he had rubbed one or two of the potatoes in his hands. 'Are they nice and dry?'

'No' bad,' I admitted. 'They're not waxy, anyway.'

'My own are, but you should see the size of them,' he

told me. 'I planted them in that boggy patch that's never been ploughed before, and I used nothin' but seaweed for them. My God! I'm tellin' you, I can tuck just one of them under my arm and it'll do a dinner for the four of us.' He gathered up one or two potoatoes that had missed the pail and put them in. 'I'd best be gettin' along, I suppose.' He sighed. 'She'll have it in for me if I'm not there on the dot.' He swung his mailbag into a more comfortable position and started off, but changing his mind he came back to stand beside me again. 'Did they tell you about yon white beast?' he enquired anxiously.

'Yes,' I admitted, with a surreptitious glance towards the hazel copse.

'Well, if you should see one be sure and chop it in two with your graipe,' he instructed, and even while I gaped at him in astonishment he dove forward and picked up something from the soil. 'That's the beastie,' he told me, triumphantly displaying on the palm of his hand a fat grub that might have been white beneath its film of earth. 'Make sure you kill it properly now or it'll play hell with your potatoes next year.'

He loped off, whistling a Gaelic air to which the thudding of the mailbag against his bottom provided an erratic accompaniment. I threw the last potato into the pail, forked the dead haulm into heaps ready for burning and, heavy with weariness yet full of satisfaction, went back to the cottage.

The kitchen was warm and while I waited for the torch, soaked in methylated spirit, to heat the tube of the pressure lamp, I looked out across the darkening bay to where the pattern of lighthouses were already flinging their charted beams over the furrowed water, the most powerful of them kindling a fleeting window-patterned reflection of itself on my kitchen wall. The lighthouses always served to emphasize the change in my life, for in town at this time in the evening it would have been the ordered queues of street lamps flicking on to contemplate the drab pavements with stark suspicious glare. I drew the peony-flowered curtains and pumped the lamp until it hissed into brightness.

The kettle was steaming on the stove when there was a rattle at the door and Morag came in. I put aside the grocery list I had been studying with its quotations for bolls (140 lb.) of flour and oatmeal, for sugar by the hundredweight, pot barley, rice and coconut by the stone, for syrup in fourteen-pound tins.

'Ach, now, seein' you doin' that reminds me Neilly was askin' me to get some of that tobacco for him,' said Morag, nodding towards the list. 'I'll not be sendin' there for a whiley yet so perhaps you'll order it along with your own,' she suggested.

I took up the list. 'What kind does he like?' I asked, having always been intrigued by the esoteric attraction of 'Black Twist', 'Bogey Roll', 'Warhorse' and 'Warlock'. To my delight she plumped for 'Bogey Roll'.

'I wonder,' I mused as I wrote it down, 'just what "Bogey Roll" has that the others haven't got?'

'Indeed I don't know,' responded Morag, 'but when he hasn't any tobacco from the shop Neilly will smoke nettle leaves, or dockens, or I've even known him stuff his pipe with brown paper and smoke it, so I shouldn't think it's anythin' particular.' She wriggled herself into her chair like a hen into a dust bath before taking the cup of tea I was holding out to her.

We sipped in silence for a while, half listening for the furtive whisperings or stealthy footsteps of children who, on their one night of jollity in the year, might be rigging a booby trap outside my door or climbing on to the roof to drop empty tins down the chimney.

'Did you hear about the sod-hut tinkers?' Morag burst out suddenly.

'No,' I admitted. 'What about them?'

'They're goin' to have a marryin',' she announced ex-ultantly, 'in the church with the minister.'

I stared at her incredulously. During the spring and summer months Bruach, in common with most of the Hebrides, was beset by tinkers selling every kind of mer-chandise and of more recent years by the collectors of scrap-iron—still called 'tinks'—who poked uninvited around our crofts and sheds discovering our assets and then, with irri-tating insistence, making offers for everything we did not wish to dispose of. I have never forgotten one filthy old man who had stood glowering at me through a draggle of grey beard while a confederate of his was glibly proposing to 'take out of my way' an old trough with which I had not the slightest intention of parting. During a slight pause the old man had jerked suddenly into the conflict by asking, 'Is they your own teeths?' with such an air of covetousness that I expected him to immediately make me an offer for them.

These 'scrap tinks' were considered by the crofters to be of a much lower class than the rest of the tinkers, largely, I think, because they indulged in no courteous Highland preamble before they got down to business, a neglect the Bruachites found distasteful. But they became, like the other 'tinks', an unavoidable adjunct to the Hebridean way of life, and in the early mornings throughout the spring and summer one could see their tents or their dejected old lorries parked in some green and pleasant spot just off the road while nearby a kettle hung over a crackling twig fire. On clear sunlit mornings when the air was splintered with birdsong and the faces of the breakfasting tinkers seemed to reflect the sunshine, the life appeared to be not without a certain glamour, but any hankering for it was dispelled on dreary mornings of storm when the camping place was sleeked by rain and dotted with dismal heaps of scrap unloaded from the lorries so as to make sleeping space for the family. There was no crackling fire then but only a pile of twigs which a drape of gloomy-faced men took turns to fan with their hats into some semblance of flame.

Bruach normally saw the last of its tinkers well before the end of September but this year a company of them had decided to stay for the winter and had built for themselves a substantial hut of sods, covered with tarpaulins which were weighted down with boulders from the bed of the burn. Although the encampment was a good two miles from the village the Bruachites at first seemed to find the presence

of the tinkers a trifle disturbing, partly, I suspected, because they could never completely dissociate them from the
stories of witchcraft and magic with which a Hebridean
child is surrounded. It soon became obvious from the blue
smoke that sprouted from a hole in the tarpaulin that the
tinkers were burning peat, so peat stacks were examined
frequently, though even had pilfering been observed it is
unlikely that anything would have been done about it except to carry all the peats home to the safety of the shed at
the side of the house. When two of the more incautious of
the villagers reported that the tinkers had opened up a
couple of hags close to their encampment the relief was
general. No one really wanted to have any cause for complaint against the tinkers. Of course, they admitted, they
had no right whatever to cut peats without permission from
the village. 'Ach, but what's a few yards of peat in hundreds
of acres of the stuff!' they exclaimed in tones that would
not have been half so tolerant had it been one of themselves who had so flouted tradition. It was exactly the same
with the driftwood on the shore. In Bruach the men went
regularly to the beaches, putting up above high-tide mark
all manner of flotsam and jetsam ranging from small pieces
of driftwood which would make good kindling to large hatch
covers which might provide solid supports for a new byre
or shed. All along the shore these dog-in-the-manger piles
of wood were dotted, constantly being added to, rarely being depleted. Sometimes the larger pieces would have ini-
tials roughly scratched on them to proclaim the finder but
this was unnecessary, for in the village it was an unwritten

law that a man owned whatever he put above high-tide mark and it was considered to be the depth of treachery for another to lay a finger on it, even if it had been lying rotting there for much of the claimant's lifetime. They were able apparently to memorize not only each heap they had gathered but each individual piece and I have witnessed an old man who had not moved from his fireside for several years describe after a few moments' meditation a piece of wood of a particular shape and size and then give an importunate relative reluctant permission to abstract it from one of his caches on the shore. Yet now came the tinkers who with smiling indifference and without a sign of remonstrance from the owners indulged in day-long sorties, looting the stores of wood with a rapacity that, had they been ordinary villagers, would have resulted in months of bitterness and recrimination.

There appeared to be at least a dozen of the 'sod-hut tinks' and from the sounds of laughter one could always hear in the vicinity of their abode they seemed to pack a great deal of jollity into their unfettered lives. The grocer reported that they were ideal customers in that they bought unstintingly, paid cash and carried their purchases away with effortless good humour. The barman was quoted as having said much the same thing.

'Which of them is going to marry which?' I enquired of Morag, being as much enchanted with the news as she was.

'I believe it's yon little one Erchy's after sayin' has the "come-to-bed eyes".' She gave a wry chuckle. 'Aye, an' I mind our own Hector tellin' him, "Well, Erchy," says he, "if it's come-to-bed eyes she has then I'm thinkin' it's a been-to-bed walk her legs has."'

'Oh, that one,' I exclaimed, recalling a young girl with rather bandy legs, bounteous chestnut hair and shadowed lazy eyes, who had called at the cottage a couple of times and with liquid mendicant chant had tried to flatter, wheedle and coax me into buying bowls and ladles made from dried milk tins, roughly soldered.

'Aye, that one,' confirmed Morag.

'And who is she marrying?' I demanded.

'And who but that one they call "Hairy Willie",' she declared with great satisfaction.

'Hairy Willie!' I ejaculated. 'But he's too old for her, and anyway he's in Canada.'

'He may be too old for her but he's not in Canada,' contradicted Morag with smug emphasis. 'He's back at the sod hut.'

I was overcome with curiosity. The rumour a month or so earlier that Hairy Willie's sister in Canada had sent him the money for a three-month trip by plane to visit her had caused a great sensation in the village. No one had at first believed the story but gradually signs of unusual excitement became apparent among the tinkers themselves. Several bachelors in the village reported having been asked for cast-off underwear to fit a 'big, big man'. (Hairy Willie was a clothes-bursting six foot two.) Others were asked if they could spare a suitcase. Then when interest had been whipped up to its peak Hairy Willie himself did Erchy the great honour of appearing at his door and asking 'would he be havin' a kind of tie or two he wasn't wantin' to go to Canada?' Erchy had obligingly produced a couple of cherished ties and in return for the gift had asked Hairy Willie point blank if the story of his flying to Canada was really true. Hairy Willie had been delighted not only to show Erchy the letter from his sister (he himself could not read) but also the money order she had enclosed for his fare. ('An' the size of it near knocked me over!' Erchy confided afterwards.)

One day the following week a bevy of tinker children was seen climbing over and under, inside and outside Hairy Willie's ramshackle old van, racing each other with pails of water from the burn, washing it and polishing it and making it fit for the journey down to Glasgow where he was to catch the plane. The very next day Hairy Willie, dressed in a lovat-green tweed jacket which had come from the Laird via the gamekeeper; a pair of homespun trousers, furtively supplied by the shepherd's tender-hearted wife; a pious black hat begged from the minister, and a pair of ex-R.A.F. flying boots from an entirely unaccountable source, had climbed into his van beside a battered portmanteau and amidst a chorus of good wishes, spurts of delighted dancing and waving of arms and hats started on his adventure. Since then the village had heard no news of him and it had been assumed by everyone that he was safely in Canada with his sister. Now, here was Morag saying that he was already back at the encampment.

'Didn't he like Canada?' I asked.

'Indeed the man never got to Canada,' she replied. 'You mind he was drivin' himself down?' I nodded. 'Well, they're tellin' me he collected that many drunken drivin' summonses on his way to Glasgow that all the money for his fare had gone on fines before ever he got there.' Morag was outraged by my laughter. 'A waste of good money,' she scolded, and then added thoughtfully, 'not but what it was a waste, anyway. How did she know he was her real brother? You canna' tell with tinks.'

'So now he's proposing to get married,' I said.

'Aye, an' it should be worth seein'. She's been around tryin' to find somebody will give her a dress for the weddin'. Indeed she was at my own house yesterday but I had nothin' would do for her.'

'Poor kid,' I said. 'I wish I could help her.'

'Ach, she's no needin' help,' replied Morag. 'Mary Anne's promised her a white dress she has by her.'

'Her own wedding dress?' I asked.

'Ach, no, mo ghaoil, it's just a dress of some sort she inhabited from her granny when she died. It's been up in a box in the loft long since.' I felt even sorrier for the girl. 'It's queer all the same,' Morag went on, 'the likes of them tinks wantin' to get marrit in a church.'

'Why?' I asked. 'How do they usually get married?' I was thinking of the traditional gypsy ceremony.

'Indeed I'm thinkin' they don't usually bother themselves,' said Morag.

There was a sudden thump on the door and it flew open, revealing a group of masked children clad in a variety of old seamen's jerseys, yachting caps, long black skirts and tattered dresses. They blundered into the kitchen and silently stood in an aura of mildew and excitement, waiting for us to guess their identities, greeting our deliberately wrong guesses with anonymous snorts and giggles and reluctantly acknowledging correct ones by removing their masks. Eventually all the masks were removed and we gave them each a threepenny bit. I put out a bowl of water in which lurked quartered apples and rolling up their voluminous sleeves the children ducked for them with eager deliberation. When the apples were finished they put on their masks again and securely tucking up flapping skirts and trouser legs ran off gaily to repeat the performance at the next house.

'I'm thinkin',' said Morag, 'the tinks will be after some of them dresses the children was wearin' tonight if they see them. They'll want to be dressin' themselves up for the weddin' as well as the bride.'

A few days after Halloween the prospective bride called at the cottage. Trying to conceal her excitement she told me wistfully that she had tried 'everywhere just' (she implied by her tones every reputable store in town) but could not get a pair of white shoes to fit her. Had I such a thing as a pair? She would be so full of thanks to me if I could but just find her a wee pair. I knew I had absolutely nothing suitable. I also knew that she would not believe me if I told her so. I invited her inside to inspect my shoe cupboard to see if there was anything else that might do. There were no light shoes at all, my Bruach footwear being limited to gumboots, brogues and carpet slippers. She smiled at me ingratiatingly. She understood, of course, I wouldn't want to part with them; they were nice anyway and that cool in the summer for the feets. I wondered at first which particular pair of shoes she was going to try to win from me and then I saw that her glance kept going to a pair of grubby old tennis shoes in the bottom of the cupboard. I bent down and rooted them out. There was a small hole in the toe of each.

'These?' I asked incredulously. 'You want these?'

Ach, it was too much to ask of me. She tried to look contrite, but her eyes returned greedily to the shabby shoes I was holding. I handed them to her.

'Have them by all means if you want them,' I said, and poking about found a tube of whitener not completely hard which I also pushed into her hand. Full of smiles and dramatic predictions of good luck that would follow my generosity she rushed off clutching the shoes to her and leaving me with an inexplicable sense of guilt which was not dissipated until Morag told me that she had heard the bride's mother only that day pestering the grocer to get her some coloured toilet rolls.

'Aye, I thought that would surprise you. I was surprised myself,' she told me, with cheerful disapproval. 'Toilet rolls for tinks!' she scoffed, 'and coloured ones at that! "What's wrong with a handful of grass the same as we use ourselves?" I says to her, and do you know what she was wantin' them for?'

I shook my head and waited.

'She said she must have coloured paper for makin' the flowers for the bucket the bride was goin' to carry.' She snorted. 'Fancy that now. Not satisfied with a white dress my fine lady must have a bucket to carry like brides in the papers and her mother's havin' to make her the flowers for it.'

An ancient dress, a pair of old tennis shoes, a bouquet of paper flowers!

I announced my intention of going to see the wedding, and NellyElly was quick to say that she would come with me if she could get someone to see to the Post Office for her. Mary Anne, delighted at the possibility of seeing the bride in her grandmother's dress, planned that she too would come if Jamie would get back from the cow in time. Morag indicated that she would come if the Lord spared her.

The day of the wedding brought a sunwhite morning encircled with gull cries and harried by a bluster of wind. The wedding was to be at twelve o'clock in a church some twelve miles distant so there was time only to rush through the morning's chores before embarking on a wrestling bout with 'Joanna', my car, who with age was becoming an increasingly slow starter. I was late and all three of my friends were walking along the road towards the cottage when I met them.

'My, they're sayin' there's tinks come from as far as Inverness for this weddin'!' exclaimed Morag as soon as we had started off.

'Indeed and so they have,' agreed NellyElly. 'Did you no' have them round yesterday just? Beggin' me to buy they were, just so they could give the bridegroom a wee bitty somethin' for his weddin'.'

'I'm knowin' fine what the wee bitty somethin' would be, too,' observed Morag sagely. 'It'll be a rough weddin' if there's many from Inverness there.'

'There's a dozen came from there yesterday,' reported NellyElly. 'An' I'm after hearin' that the little boy they brought with them was a wee monster. He was swearin' that bad on the train they had to lock him in the guard's van all the way.' She sucked in a horrified breath. 'Folks was sayin' they'd never heard anythin' like it.'

'If there's a dozen of them from Inverness there's as many from other places,' put in Mary Anne. 'There must be near forty of them all together in that sod hut. Dear knows where they're all to sleep.'

'Ach, they'll no' be carin' where they sleep,' said Morag disdainfully. 'An' they'll have that much drink inside them they won't know where they are anyway.'

'Erchy was past their camp yesterday and he was sayin' there was good smells for a mile either way,' supplied NellyElly. 'They were after cookin' the chickens they got. He says they had three or four fires goin' and he reckoned they had about fifteen birds there of one sort or another. They're doin' well out of it. I know the cockerel my mother gave them was near as big as a goose.'

'My own was as big,' countered Morag with pride. 'I was thinkin' maybe I'd keep him till the New Year, but ach, when they asked me would they get somethin' for the weddin' feast I felt I'd best give it to them.' She smoothed her gloves complacently. 'All the same,' she went on, 'I believe they've done well for meat from Lachy's cow that fell over the cliff a day or two back. He says they were runnin' back and fro with pails and basins to it all day long till the tide took it away.'

'Indeed I heard that too,' confirmed Mary Anne. 'So I didn't give them a bird at all. I wasn't for givin' them anythin' at first but the hens are layin' well just now so Jamie said to give them a few eggs.'

'Somebody told me you gave them a pound of tea, too!' accused Morag.

'Aye,' admitted Mary Anne self-consciously. 'I had plenty so I thought I'd not be missin' it.'

'I'm glad everyone didn't give them a chicken,' I said, regretting that I had put only half a crown into the toe of each of the tennis shoes.

'Why do you say that?' asked Morag.

'Because I didn't,' I replied.

'Ach, well, I daresay you gave them eggs or potatoes or somethin',' she suggested. 'There was no call for everybody to give them chickens.'

'I didn't give them anything at all,' I confessed. 'The bride asked me for a pair of old tennis pumps I had and when I gave them to her I popped half a crown into the toe of each of them, but I wasn't asked to contribute anything to the feast.'

'No indeed, and that was plenty to give them,' comforted Nelly Elly. 'They were havin' a struggle to carry home the food they collected when I saw them. What with all they'd have from Lachy's cow and them havin' got a whole sack of potatoes from Roddy they'll be feedin' like kings and queens anyway—not but what they don't always,' she added.

'Better than the rest of us,' agreed Morag, with a tremor of indignation. 'An' not only that. Did you hear how he's been gettin' the petrol so they can go for a honeymoon?'

We all admitted that we had not heard.

'Why, he's been takin' his van to a different spot each day an' there he leaves it an' stands himself beside it with an empty can. He stops every car and lorry as it comes by an' tells them he's run out of petrol and asks will he get a bit to see him home.' She paused for our exclamations. 'Some of the drivers feels that sorry for him they'll give him near a canful,' she continued, 'an' my fine fellow has a fifty-gallon drum in the back of his van so as soon as they're out of sight he nips round an' puts the petrol into it.'

'Oh, my, my, he's the wily one,' chuckled Mary Anne appreciatively.

'Hear that now!' said NellyElly with envy-tinged disapproval. 'What will those tinks be after thinkin' of next?'

'I wonder?' I murmured, as I was assailed by a sudden recollection. 'I wonder if that's what he was up to the other day when Hamish saw him, broken down, as he thought, beside the road?'

'Likely it was,' said Morag.

I started to chuckle as I recounted for the amusement of my companions the story Hamish had told me. It seemed he had been walking back to Bruach after delivering some

sheep to the mainland when he had come across Hairy
Willie, looking rather grimier and sweatier than usual,
bending over the engine of his van. When Hamish had
drawn alongside the tinker had proceeded to give him a
brief but vitriolic description of the misdeameanours of the
ancient engine and while he was in full spate a car drew up
and a gentleman got out to ask if help was needed. Hairy
Willie promptly replied that it was 'Nothin' but a wee bitty
petrol she was after wantin'.' But the gentleman, according
to Hamish, had already started his own investigation and,
to the tinker's very obvious surprise, had discovered that
the tank contained ample petrol. He had continued his ex-
amination of the engine, poking and prodding, screwing
and unscrewing, and eventually he had told Hairy Willie
to try to start it. The engine had responded to the first pull.
The mystified expression of the tinker had changed to one
of such relief that the gentleman had asked anxiously if he
had been stranded for long and how far away his home lay,
to which questions Hairy Willie replied with his custom-
ary glib mendacity. 'Thank you, thank you, sir,' he repeated
again and again. 'What would I have done now if yourself
hadn't come along?'

'It isn't I you should thank but God Almighty,' replied
the gentleman. 'It is He who sent me here to help you.'

'Hairy Willie's face looked as though he had two
tongues and had bitten both of them,' Hamish reported,
'an' he turned to the man. "You must be a minister," says
he. "I am indeed," says the man. "Is there anything wrong
with that?" "Wrong!" shouts Hairy Willie. "Wrong? Man!

Why the bloody hell didn't you tell me you was a minister, I might have started swearin' in front of you".'

My companions exchanged looks before they permitted themselves to giggle demurely.

By this time we were rounding the head of the loch where the wet, black hills gloomed over acres of shore which the tide had left to a shifting mosaic of seabirds. Hooded crows swaggered uneasily among the fringes of salt weed and an occasional heron stood in aristocratic aloofness, with feathered 'widow's weeds' lifting gently in the breeze.

'Here comes the boys!' announced Morag, and I drew in to the side of the road. There had been a cattle sale at the loch side that morning and the Bruach men had started out at two o'clock to walk their cattle to it. They were trudging their long way back now, driving before them either cattle they had bought at the sale or cattle they had refused to sell because of poor prices. Morag put down the window. 'How did the sale go, boys?' she demanded eagerly.

'No' bad,' they admitted.

'Good prices?'

'Ach, no' bad.'

'What did our own Ruari make on his beasts?' It was not done to ask a man outright what he got for his cattle. You asked him about a neighbour's or a friend's beasts and hoped he would volunteer to tell you how he himself had fared.

'I believe he got seventy for the two of them.'

'The dear knows!' exclaimed Morag noncommittally. 'An' is he after buyin' a beast in for himself?'

'Aye,' was the disdainful reply. 'A right queer beastie, too, that looks as if it's been crossed with a camel.'

'The fool!' said Morag with derision. She turned her attention to wee Shamus, who at eight years old had achieved the status of manhood by being allowed to walk his widowed mother's cow through the night to the sale. His valiant efforts to disguise his tiredness were not helped by the fact that he had a black and swollen eye.

'Shamus!' Morag taxed him. 'You've not been fightin', surely?'

'I have not then,' replied Shamus with flushed stubbornness.

'You haven't? Then how is it you have such a black eye?'

Shamus kicked his gumbooted feet in the grass. 'Well, you see,' he said profoundly, 'somebody struck somebody.' But before she could question him further he had darted off to turn a cow who was trying to dodge past him.

Erchy, red-faced with exertion, came hurrying up to the car. 'Here,' he told us, 'I'm thinkin' I'll come back with you.'

'You will not,' we told him. 'We're cramped enough as it is.'

'I could sit on top,' he coaxed.

'No.' We were adamant.

'Ach, well, I'm comin' back tonight yet,' he told us as we were moving off. 'I'm feelin' I need a good drink after all the runnin' about I'm after doin' today.'

'You'll be needin' your bed, more likely,' Morag said, but he too was running to head off a recalcitrant cow.

113

'If they get the Bruach men with their cattle money and the tinkers after the weddin' they'll have a wild night at the bar tonight,' she prophesied.

We arrived at the church a little before twelve, but though there was a fair number of people standing in coy groups outside the church they were obviously not the wedding party. I pulled Joanna in behind a parked van close to the church gates before I realized with a shock that it was an ambulance. With a look of dazed enquiry I turned to Morag. Bruach modes of transport were often wildly unorthodox but surely, I thought, not an ambulance for a bride!

'Ach, no,' Morag reassured me. 'Likely it's the driver himself come to take a look at the weddin'.'

'We'll not go into the church, will we?' asked NellyElly.

'Why not?' I replied. 'I thought that was why we came.'

'Ach, no indeed, I could never go into the church with the tinks,' she giggled.

'You're not goin' in yourself, are you, Miss Peckwitt?' Mary Anne enquired.

'If Miss Peckwitt's goin' in I'll go along with her,' said Morag venturesomely.

'Of course I'm going in,' I said, and getting out of the car made for the church door, whither they all followed me with eager resignation.

Just as we reached the entrance someone shouted, 'Here they come!' and pausing to look back along the road we saw the disordered procession of tinkers coming towards us. The bride and all the female tinkers, frequently impinging on one another as they walked, headed the procession, while the groom with the equally undisciplined male tinkers followed close on their heels. Untrammelled children dove in and out with a liveliness that was in no way affected by their lengthy walk.

A thought struck me. 'What happened about the bouquet?' I enquired. 'Did the grocer get any coloured toilet rolls?'

'Not him,' replied NellyElly. 'Why would he do that when it's just left with them he'll be?'

'Did she manage to get hold of some coloured paper, then?'

'Well, indeed but didn't Enac and Fiona go over to the mainland to get themselves some boots last week, an' them feelin' that sorry for the tinker girl not gettin' her bucket they went into all the hotel lavatories and took a bit. They even went through the train while it was in the station and took some of them paper towels. Aye, but the old tinker body was well pleased when they gave it to her. The girls was well pleased too because she told them they'd have rich husbands and good luck for the rest of their lives through it.' She chuckled. 'Ach, but the men are sayin' we're all goin' daft over this weddin'.'

Distinct sounds of hilarity were now reaching us from the distance, but as they neared the church the tinkers hushed their children and their own voices and allowed their features to resume the masks of mendicancy we knew so well.

We slipped into the church and took our seats on a back pew and, taking courage from our example, most of the onlookers followed suit. So quickly did the church fill that when the tinkers arrived there were only a few front pews vacant. Embarrassed and bewildered, they squeezed themselves in, waiting vainly under the unrelenting eye of the minister to be told what to do. Hairy Willie came in and stood surveying the congregation with an artificially induced benignity. He was resplendent in his 'Canadian trip' clothes, his battered black hat being crushed under his arm. His normally shaggy hair had been cropped so close to his head that it looked as though he was wearing a nylon skull cap. Morag nudged me.

'I believe that's the haircut all the men is gettin' in Glasgow,' she whispered. 'I believe they call it the "cruel cut".'

The minister beckoned and in response Hairy Willie and his best man loped eagerly up the aisle towards him shaking the minister's decorum perceptibly. He fended them off with a rigidly held prayer-book and indicated where they should stand. Hairy Willie complied and stood with his hands clasped nonchalantly behind him. There was a hissing in the front pews and the bridegroom turned round and bestowed on his supporters a jaunty smile accompanied by a convivial wink to which they responded with such uninhibited whisperings that the minister, no doubt apprehensive of blasphemy, spoke to him quietly. Hairy Willie obligingly faced the chancel and stood to attention until perhaps recalling that the black hat crushed to shapelessness under his arm had been given to him by the minister, he reached for it and, holding it behind his back, proceeded to remould it to its original shape.

The stir of excitement that always precedes the entrance of the bride was by no means lacking at this wedding. One of the tinker children who had no doubt been held captive to this moment in the porch burst through the door, ran up the aisle and pummelling his two fists into the bridegroom's broad back yelled, 'She's comin' for ye!' He was quickly seized by a tinker at the end of the pew and pushed protestingly out of sight among the packed bodies, and all eyes turned towards the door as the bride appeared holding determinedly on to the arm of a vacillating old man who I at once recognized to be a spruced-up version of the tinker who had coveted my teeth.

I was astonished. She looked as pretty as any young bride I had ever seen. The warmhearted Mary Anne had not only washed and bleached her grandmother's dress but had re-made it so that the bodice fitted perfectly and the long skirt draped itself to conceal all but the toes of my old tennis shoes which peeped out a little dustily as she walked. Her bouquet, which she held in front of her much as a housewife might hold a flue-brush, was most artistic, though the green foliage betrayed itself by its hygenic pallor. As she walked up the aisle she turned to smile with delighted appraisal at the congregation on either side of her. She looked radiant and I do not think there was a single person present who was not extremely touched by the whole event.

VI. *Rescues*

ERCHY WAS MUCKING OUT his cow-byre when I called on him to ask if I could borrow his saw.

'My God! but I had a good laugh out of them tinks the night of the weddin',' he said.

I looked at him searchingly. Erchy had been to a cattle sale on the day of the tinkers' wedding and on such occasions his stories of subsequent happenings were not usually very lucid, due to his own inebriation.

'Aye,' he went on. 'That Hairy Willie was as drunk as I don't know what an' when one of them pulled his trousers away from his backside an' poured a pint of beer down inside Hairy Willie didn't even feel it.' Erchy leaned on his fork and smiled out at the pewter-grey sea.

'What I'd like to know is whether they got away on their honeymoon as they were supposed to?' I asked. 'There were quite a few people here who didn't believe they'd ever get away.'

'He got started all right,' said Erchy.

'Where was his bride?' I asked.

'I believe she was with him some of the time,' replied Erchy after a moment of doubt. 'Ach, but she was drunk as he was himself.' He threw out a couple more forkfuls of manure. 'I was tellin' you about them gettin' started on their honeymoon.'

I nodded.

'Aye, well we all saw him go, with his bride sittin' beside him. He set off an' he was drivin' all over the road. It's a damty good thing the pollis knew to keep out of the way or they would have had to take him in. The rest of the tinks was laughin' and dancin' away in front of the hotel. Honest, I didn't want to get drunk myself, I was enjoyin' watchin' them so much.' He looked a little wistful. 'I can tell you I saved myself a packet of money that way too,' he added. 'Did I not, Cailleach?' I turned to see that his mother had come up behind us. She smiled warmly at the two of us. 'I wish you could be always savin' your monies like that,' she chided him gently, for he was the apple of her eye and she did not really begrudge him his occasional wildnesses. 'You'll see and take a wee strupak with me before you go,' she said to me and I promised that I would.

'I was tellin' Miss Peckwitt about the tinkers' honeymoon,' Erchy told her.

'Oh, my, my,' whispered his mother disapprovingly. 'It was terrible just, was it not?'

'Why, what happened?' I asked with mounting curiosity.

'Well,' said Erchy, continuing with his story. 'About an hour after they'd gone we was sittin' in the kitchen of the hotel havin' a bite of somethin' to eat with the cook, for it was well past closin' time. There comes a bangin' on the door and when the cook goes to open it, there on the step is Hairy Willie. "For God's sake, help me!" he bursts out. "Here, here," she says to him. "Help you what way?" for she thinks he's still pretty drunk. "To get my van out of the ditch," he tells her. "Find me some men and some ropes before the pollis sees it." "How did it get into the ditch?" she asks him. "Woman," says he, "I'm thinkin' I must have put it there myself," he says, "an' now the bloody thing's turned right over." The cook brings him in to the kitchen an' she was tellin' him how lucky he was that we were all there still. Ruari and one or two of the others went off to see would they find a rope. Suddenly the cook says to Hairy Willie, "Where's your bride?" "My bride?" says he as though he's never heard of her before that minute. "Yes, indeed," said the cook, "the girl you married today in the church and was with you in the van." "Ach!" Hairy Willie tells her, as though it doesn't matter, "she's still under the van." "Still under the van?" the cook screams at him. "My God! what are you thinkin' of? You should never have left her. All you're thinkin' about is gettin' your old van out of the ditch before the pollis sees it, when that poor lassie might be lyin' there dead." Hairy Willie looked at her as though she's goin' daft. "I know fine she's not dead," he tells her. "I could hear her swearin' after me all the way along the road."'

121

'Oh, the monster!' gasped Erchy's mother in horrified tones.

'Ruari had the hotel car out by then,' continued Erchy with unabated enthusiasm. 'An' when we got to the place there was Willie's van upside down in the ditch with half of a stone dyke on top of it that he'd knocked down. There was no sound from the van so we told Willie he must talk to the girl and see if she was all right.' Erchy's eyes glittered with remembered amusement. 'As soon as he opened his mouth there was such a stream of swearin' would have turned your stomach to hear it. From a lassie, too.' He succeeded in looking shocked.

'Dear only knows,' murmured his mother piously.

'Anyway,' he went on, 'we got the van out an' the lassie was all right seemingly, only drunk still.'

'Well, thank goodness for that,' I said with a chuckle.

'Wait you,' warned Erchy. 'I haven't finished yet.'

I looked at him expectantly and his mother put a hand over her mouth in an effort to hide a smile.

'We'd hardly got the van out but the fellow who has the croft came shoutin' at us. He'd seen all the lights and he'd been wonderin' what was happenin'. When he sees his wall's all broken down, by God! there was more swearin' and cursin' from him. "My cows will get out through that," he shouts at Hairy Willie, "an' if they get lost it's you that will pay for them. And you'll pay for me to mend that hole in the dyke," says he, "or I'll have the pollis on you." Hairy Willie was that scared I believe I could hear his moustache rattlin'. "Where's your cows now?" he asks the man. "In there," says the man, pointin' to the dyke, "but as soon as they find this hole they'll be through it. You'll just stay yourself and see that they don't get out." Hairy Willie was lookin' that bad I felt sorry for him right enough. An' then, before anybody knew what he was at, he got into his van, started it up and ran it straight back into the ditch again so that it filled up the gap in the dyke. "There," he tells the man, "will that not keep your cattle in?" "Aye," says the man, and you should have seen the look on his face. Then he starts to laugh. "All right," he tells Hairy Willie. "Seein' my cattle's safe I'll not say any more about it," and he went off home.'

'And what happened to the tinkers then?' I asked.

'Ach, they was just goin' off back to their camp, holdin' each other up, the last I saw of them,' said Erchy, as he bent to lift a spilling forkful of manure. 'I expect that's where they're goin' to spend the honeymoon if there's room for them to get in yet.'

I went back to the house with Erchy's mother, had my strupak and collected the saw, which she seemed a little hesitant to give me. It was not until I was on my way home that I realized it was a Saturday and that she would have preferred to keep the saw in her own house until the Monday so that there should be no possibility of its being used upon the Sabbath day.

'What are you goin' to do with that, now?' asked the grocer facetiously, when I went to buy a tin of meat from him. 'Build yourself a new house, are you?'

'I'm going to have a good go at those old blackcurrant

bushes,' I told him. 'They never produce a crop and I think it's because there's too much old wood there.'

'I wouldn't be surprised,' said the grocer with only tepid interest. 'Did your butcher meat not come that you're buyin' a tin of meat on a Saturday?' he asked curiously.

'I didn't order any this week,' I told him. 'That tink they call Phillibeag promised he'd bring a rabbit for me for the weekend, but I doubt if I'll get it now.'

'Ach, you're better not to get anythin' from that man anyway,' the grocer warned me. 'He wouldn't care what sort of a beast he'd sell you. Why, they tell me if he finds a cat in his snares he just skins it and sells it along with his rabbits. He says folks can't tell the difference.'

'Oh Lord!' I said, and my appetite even for tinned meat vanished completely.

'You'd be as well to keep some tins of meat in the house in case we get snow,' the grocer counselled. 'It's lookin' as though it's not far off.'

'Oh, surely not yet,' I said, thinking of my meagre fuel supply.

'Aye, indeed. My brother was sayin' only last night he was seein' plenty of that thick snow waitin' at the back of the hills. It'll be here before long, likely.'

His prediction had me a little worried and as I hurried home I mentally reviewed the contents of my store cupboard and the quantity of feeding stuffs left in the barn. I resolved to write once again to the coal merchant to ask him to speed up the delivery of coal I had ordered some time ago. So engrossed was I in my calculations that although I was vaguely aware of a male figure approaching I was not shocked into the realization that it was a stranger until I saw him take out a large white handkerchief and blow his nose on it. Recollecting myself in time to stifle the usual chaffing remark or specific comment on the weather I wished him 'Good afternoon', to which he replied with stilted cordiality and continued on his way. I was curious. Now that the tourist season was over any stranger in the village was usually something to do with an official body so that it was almost a duty for everyone to discover the reason for their visit. I turned into Morag's cottage to find her in the act of taking a large steaming dumpling off the fire.

'I've just seen a strange man!' I announced.

'A strange man?' echoed Morag and Behag together and even little Fiona stopped trying to tie the tails of two cats together to stand and stare at me in unblinking surprise.

'Who would that be, I wonder?' went on Morag. 'It's late for anyone to be here. What like was he?'

I described him as well as I could.

'Had he an open or a closed collar?' demanded Morag.

The expression was new to me and I had to ask her what she meant. 'I mean, did he have a closed collar like a minister or an open collar like a tourist?' she explained.

'Open,' I said.

'Ach, well, then, likely he'll be that student fellow has been preachin' at the Seceder church these three Sundays past,' interpreted Morag. 'He'll be stayin' with Kirsty, the poor mannie.'

'That'll be the one that Euan was praising up so much?' suggested Behag with a titter.

'Aye, he will be indeed,' agreed Morag, a reciprocal smile on her lips.

'Does Euan go to the other church now?' I asked in surprise. Euan, the half-wit brother of 'Padruig the Daftie' had, until recent months, been kept away from any church because of the profanity of his language. However the two female 'pilgrims', to whom I have referred in a previous book,* found in Euan not only a devoted admirer but also a proselyte who made up in susceptibility for what he lacked in intelligence. During their relatively short stay in the village they had undertaken both his lay and his religious education with such a degree of success that he no longer referred to a chicken as a 'feathery bugger' but was content to indulge his passion for epithets by the use of such mildnesses as 'that damned-by-God hen'. They had even taught him to sing a hymn and now whenever one passed by Padruig's cottage the lusty voice of Euan could be heard rendering adagio, prestissimo, pianissimo or fortissimo, the words of 'When He Cometh' with tuneless assiduity. It was shortly after the departure of the 'pilgrims' that Padruig had been taken ill and had gone to be nursed by his married sister on the mainland. Euan had shortly afterwards asserted his right to go to church and there he had since attended regularly, sitting in his pew rigid with importance except when the hymns were announced when, handing his book to a neighbour, he would request that the right hymn

*See *The Sea for Breakfast*.

126

should be found for him, although he could not read a single word. When the singing commenced no matter what the hymn might be Euan joined in vociferously with 'When He Cometh', remaining aloofly indifferent to the nudgings and objurgations of those in close proximity.

'Euan's been goin' to the other church for three or four weeks past now,' Morag told me. 'There's no tellin' my fine lad what he's to do now that Padruig's not keepin' the upper hand of him.'

'Why has he left your church?' I asked her.

'The dear knows why,' she replied, 'unless it's just that he's feelin' he needs a change.' She cut off a large hunk of hot dumpling and wrapped it in a cloth for me to take home for my supper.

'I really must ask Euan next time I see him why he's changed churches,' I told them as I said goodbye. 'It would be interesting to hear what he has to say.'

It was not until the following Monday afternoon when I was returning from a session of beachcombing that I met Euan. He too had been beachcombing and the creel on his back was piled high with driftwood. I complimented him on his industry and then went on to question him about his apostasy. 'It's quite a long way further for you to have to walk to your new church,' I suggested.

'Yes, Missed,' he agreed eagerly. 'But when I gets there it's a nice carpet I have to my feets an' a good stove to warm me. I's not goin' to shiver in that dirty old church when I can go a bit further an sit back like a gentleman.' He leaned the creel against the dyke, folded his arms in front of him and adopted the pose of a stiff Victorian gentleman.

'What about the new student preacher,' I asked him. 'Is he good?'

'God's hell!' he exclaimed with blasphemous piety. 'I believe he has the Lord in him okay.'

'You enjoy his sermons, then?'

'God's hell, but he's a good preacher!' reiterated Euan passionately.

The evening grew increasingly cold and towards night-fall a boorish wind, laden with sleet, sent everyone hurry-ing to find their cattle and chase them into their stalls for the night. The following morning I awoke to find my bed-room full of a strange pale light and when I went to the window I found the hills masked with snow with only a few dark patches pricking the sheet-white moors where the most robust heather clumps had shrugged through the thick mantle. I fed Bonny and drove her out through the moor gate where with the wisdom of her breed she would nose at the snow until she could get at the heather beneath. For a few minutes I leaned on the gate, watching the sluggish dark clouds piling themselves around the startlingly white hills and thinking how strange it was that snow, which falls so white and clean, should yet be heralded by such a dirty-looking mess of cloud. In the Hebrides snow, when it comes, assumes a recognizable personality. There is that which steals in with ballerina lissomeness on a north wind to leave the hills poised and breathless as a corps de ballet awaiting the re-entry of their star. By comparison the snow that the

south wind brings is clumsy and sluttish and lies dispirit-
edly over the land until it abandons it to slime and drab-
ness. Then there is the noisy, second-hand snow that has
been wrested off the mountains by a tyrannic gale and is
flung at us in crisp particles that needle into our skin.

There came a muffled flurry of wind threaded with
snowflakes and I hurried home to get the byre cleaned and
hay put out in readiness for Bonny's evening feed, for she
would need to be brought in earlier than usual. Despite the
cold I was glad to be outdoors, for between the snow show-
ers, which became more reticent as the day progressed, the
sun smiled benignly, the snow shimmered and above the
silence of the land came the tinkling whisper of the wind-
ruffled water. Immediately after a late lunch I went to collect Bonny for, though the last snow shower had been hardly
more than the flick of an angel's duster, as evening approached there was an increasing frostiness in the air and
already there was a rasping under my boots as I slithered
along the path from which my own and Bonny's footprints
of the morning had been obliterated. It was a nuisance having to go out on the moors to bring home a cow, though
there was solace in the beauty of the shadow-edged loch,
coldly blue except where it reflected a few tatters of an elu-
sive sunset, and in the sight of Rhuna tip-tilting its corners
up from the water like a smiling mouth, an accepted sign
of frost. But when one knew that nearly everyone else's cattle
needed only to hear a once-bellowed invitation or even the
clang of a moor gate to go hurrying through to their byres
where shelter, hay and a warm 'potach' awaited them, and

that even those cows which did not enjoy the luxury of a byre would range themselves hungrily along the fence waiting for their owners to bring them hay, it was infuriating to have to go and seek my own cosseted cow. Cows are perverse creatures and for some curious reason Bonny and Morag's cow Milky and Tearlaich's Bracty had of late formed a passionate attachment for one another, with the result that every evening, whatever the weather, we three unfortunate owners had to trudge out to the moors, separate three reluctant cows and coerce them homewards through three separate gates. Morag and Tearlaich were already making their way towards the loving trio when I reached the moor and they waited for me to join them.

'Ach, but there's no sense in this weather, no sense at all,' grumbled Morag as we got behind the cows and started them moving towards the fence. 'Me feets gets that cold, though I have on three pairs of stockings under them an' it hurts to take off my boots. I'm wishin' sometimes I could be goin' to bed in them.'

'You should put cow dung mixed with a wee bitty straw in your boots first,' advised Tearlaich. 'Aye, aye, aye, cow dung. That's what I said, cow dung.' Tearlaich was always known as 'Tearlaich-a-Tri' because of his habit of repeating a thing three times before he could be sure he had said it.

'Is that what you use yourself?' Morag asked him with a show of surprise.

'Aye, I do, I do, I do,' he replied. 'An' I'm no' after feelin' the cold a wee bitty, not a wee bit, I say.'

'I wouldn't fancy washing your socks,' I murmured.

'Socks? You dunna' need socks at all, at all; no, not at all.'

'Then surely your feets must be awful tender,' suggested Morag.

Indignantly Tearlaich turned on her and proceeded to instruct her in the acquiring of a pair of warm and comfortable feet. I gave scant attention to their conversation, being engrossed in tracing the pattern of shrew prints that interlaced one another on the snow like the strands of a necklace. The three cows were lumbering along in front of us, their great bellies bumping from time to time and their protesting moos mingling with the grumbling of the snow as it packed down beneath their hooves.

Suddenly I became conscious of a thick sucking splash just in front of us and of Tearlaich shouting in Gaelic. I looked up just in time to see the hind-quarters of Morag's cow disappearing into a bog. Panic-stricken I ran forward with the others, urging the cow to extricate herself before she sank deeper. The beast's two front feet were still on ground that seemed firm enough but as we tried to drive her forward by slaps and prods, by pulls on her horns and by continuous malediction from Tearlaich her hind-quarters only sank deeper and deeper. We bared our arms and plunged them into the bog, trying to grasp a leg and aid her in her struggles but despite our efforts the cow only seemed to settle herself until she was in the ludicrous position of sitting upright with her forelegs stretched out in front of her, like a begging dog.

'I doubt we're only makin' things worse,' panted Morag. 'We'd best go an' get help.'

We paused dejectedly for a moment, assessing the situation. It looked as if it should have been easy enough to extricate the beast when she already had two feet on firm ground but the bog was a narrow hole and by now her hindquarters were deeply embedded. Morag, looking white and strained, swept the hair from her eyes with a peaty arm. The light would not last much longer and by the time we got help from the village the cow might have lost the will to live.

'You and Miss Peckwitt had best take your own cows home,' Morag advised in desperation. 'You can get help then, while I stay here with my beast.' Tearlaich said he would put his beast 'through the gate just', but I raced Bonny home in record time. However by the time I had made my first plea for help Tearlaich had told Morag's deaf brother Ruari who had simply raised his voice and acquainted the whole village with the news. When I got back to the moor there were half a dozen men with ropes and boards in attendance round the cow, who had become distinctly more apathetic than she had been when I left. With much excited Gaelic argument and much impedance from excited dogs, a rope was tied to the cow's horns and boards were pushed down into the bog to try and give her a firm footing. But by now the cow had lost the will to struggle and the position began to look hopeless.

'Give her a dose of whisky,' suggested Ian. 'I have some here in my pocket.'

'Here, no,' said Murdoch. 'I'll drink that myself. Wait till you get the beast out before you give her the whisky and make sure it won't be wasted.'

'Ach, give her some anyway,' insisted Ian, and a generous dose was poured down the cow's throat. This was followed by several more fruitless attempts to heave her out, but the struggle became increasingly difficult as what had at first been firm ground softened under the continuous treading and slithering of many feet. Even the boards which had been placed under the cow's front hooves had become slimy so that they now provided only a treacherous foothold. The men were becoming tired.

'I doubt we'll not get her out,' said Morag with weary despair.

'She has such small hooves for the size of her, that's what's the trouble,' said Murdoch. 'If she had a good big foot that wouldn't cut into the ground we maybe might get her out.'

There was a general shaking of heads in abandonment of the cow's prospects, and yet I knew they would not leave her while there was the remotest chance of her survival. I turned to see Johnny Comic, who must have been ceilidhing in the village and who now stood forlornly among the group of helpers. He suddenly looked about him, lumbered over to a small hillock and sat down. Then he proceeded to take off his very large boots. I was still staring at him perplexedly when he got up and walked through the snow towards the cow, holding out his boots.

'Here,' he told the men, 'put my boots on the poor creature's feets.'

Murdoch stared at him, bereft of speech for a moment,

and Johnny, thinking they were going to refuse, bent down and struggled the cow's front hooves into each of his boots. 'Give her a pull now,' he instructed, and derisive but obedient the men pulled. There seemed to be a slight sound from the bog. Immediately everyone became excited. 'Take off your own boots, Murdoch, you old bodach, you have the biggest feets here. See an' give us your boots an' we'll try will we get her out with them.' Almost bodily they carried the old man over to the hillock and took off his boots and then, returning to the cow, they plunged their arms into the bog once more and lifted. The bog seemed to release its hold a little more and the cow, feeling the firmness of Johnny's boots on her front hooves, heaved her body again. Everyone became cautiously jubilant. 'Be ready with them boots!' shouted someone. 'When we give her another heave see can you get them on to her feets.' They heaved altogether, the cow responded and there was a shout of triumph as her hind-quarters suddenly came up out of the bog. Murdoch's boots were jammed on her hind hooves, and with boots on all four feet she was pulled and pushed to firm ground.

'Ach, but she's in a pretty bad way,' said Ian, as the cow swayed from side to side and looked as though she would fall back into the bog. 'Get her a wee bit further away and give her another dose of whisky, that'll warm her,' he instructed. With men on either side of her to prevent her falling over the cow was persuaded slowly forward. 'Now, pour this down her throat,' said Ian. I think it was Erchy who seized the bottle and, making a pouch of the cow's mouth, poured down the rest of the spirit.

'By God!' he said to Morag and me as we rubbed the cow with handfuls of the hay someone had brought, 'that was a damty queer place for a cow to be. How did she get there?'

There followed a great deal of explaining until there came a shout from Murdoch who was still sitting on the hillock, trying to cradle first one foot and then the other in order to keep it warm. Johnny Comic seemed hardly to notice the loss of his boots.

'How am I goin' to get home without gettin' my death of cold?' demanded Murdoch irately. 'Somebody had best go and get my Sunday boots and bring them to me.'

'Tearlaich will go, an' he'll fill them with dung for you first,' returned Morag, laughing now with relief

'Here, no!' expostulated Murdoch. 'They'll not let me into the house.'

'You'd best get that beast movin',' Ian told us, seeing the cow shivering with cold and fright. 'Miss Peckwitt, give the cow a wind to see will it start her off,' he commanded me.

'A wind?' I repeated stupidly.

'Aye, indeed so.' He leaped over the bog and pushing me aside seized the cow's tail which he began to crank as though it were the starting handle of a car. Whether it was the maltreatment of her tail or a sudden bellow from Tearlaich's cow on the other side of the fence that provided the impetus I do not know but the beast gave an answering bellow, lunged forward and started to lumber erratically away from us.

'By God, she's drunk! I must have given the beast too much whisky,' shouted Erchy with a jubilation that was tempered by horror.

'By God, but she has on my boots!' shouted Murdoch. 'Take them from the beast before they're lost to me.' But no one heeded him for the relief of tension had brought laughter and shrill comments and also an awareness of our cold and tired bodies.

If a stranger had seen our procession that night as it wound its way over the still moors that were silvered with moonlight and in the wake of a drunken cow wearing tackety boots, with one bootless old man being carried 'piggy back' by big Ian and the other trudging in his stockinged feet through the snow, he surely must have thought we were engaged in some pagan ritual. As Erchy put it, 'It's a damty good thing this didn't happen in the summer when there's folks about or they'd have said we was as mad as I don't know what.'

The snow lasted for nearly three weeks, and every day the sun shone brilliantly during the brief hours of daylight and then sank in an extravagant splendour of gold and crimson that rippled and pulsed across the sky.

'How about a trip in Hector's boat tomorrow?' Erchy asked me one day as I was breaking the ice that formed each night on the water butts.

'I'd love to,' I said with alacrity.

'There's a message come through to the Post Office that the folks over at the Glen is gettin' short of food an' they canna' get to them by road yet. NellyElly was askin' would Hector take some there tomorrow.'

The snow had made it impossible to use any sort of vehicle even on the Bruach road and so Hector and Erchy and Duncan, the post mistress's son, were well loaded with parcels of every shape and size when they passed the cottage on their way down to the boat. Morag and Behag, grumbling good-naturedly, shuffled behind them carrying their own offerings of homebaked oatcakes and scones in a sack thrown over the shoulder and held there with one hand. The other hand shielded their eyes from the sparkling brightness of the snow. I plodded after them, resting my eyes from the brilliance of the land by looking out to sea where *Ealasaid*, Hector's new boat, lay serenely at her moorings, at this distance looking like an ivory carving set in a polished sea. On closer inspection the effect was spoiled by the girdle of old motor-tyres with which she was draped, for though boats are ever more elaborately equipped and piers are ever more elaborately designed the fishermen still raid the shores and village dumps for old motor-tyres to prevent the two from becoming too familiar.

It was bitterly cold up in the bow of the boat where I chose to stand, but had I gone aft I should have been forced to breathe the fumes from the fo'c'sle fire which Morag was already lighting. Erchy noticed my teeth chattering.

'I don't know why you don't go in there with Behag and Morag,' he chided me. 'You'll be after gettin' perished with the cold out here.'

I indicated my binoculars. 'I want to keep a watch out for the deer,' I explained. 'This weather will have driven them down to the shore, don't you think?'

'Aye,' agreed Erchy morosely. 'But what good is it goin' to do you to see the deer, anyway?'

'I'm just interested,' I said.

'I'll give you a shout if I see them,' he promised. 'Now for God's sake, woman, go down into the fo'c'sle before you freeze to death in front of my eyes.'

The fo'c'sle was damp and odorous and untidily snug, the bunks full of a jumble of tarpaulins and sails and ropes, while two or three elegant whisky glasses co-existed happily with a collection of enamel cups and plates. Morag had the folding table erected so that she and Behag could sort through the more homely women's magazines which comprise the library of so many Scottish fishing boats. The table itself had intrigued me from the first time I saw it, for though it was made of only two rough and many-knotholed boards, six of the best-placed knotholes had been knocked out to provide the crew with some of the most stable egg-cups ever devised.

'Here's your deer!' shouted Erchy appearing momentarily in the entrance and I scrambled up on deck to see a herd of deer, apprehensive and poised for flight yet reluctant to leave the kelp on which they had been feeding.

'I can count three stags and twelve hinds,' I turned ecstatically to Erchy. 'How many can you see, Erchy?'

He flicked an unenthusiastic glance towards the shore and then huddled back into the wheelhouse with Hector.

'Erchy!' I reproached him. 'Aren't you interested in the deer?'

'The only deer I'm interested in just now is piping hot on a plate,' he retorted with a nod of dismissal.

I returned to the fo'c'sle and my two still-engrossed companions and after about twenty minutes we heard the engine note of the boat change as she was put out of gear.

'We must be there,' said Morag, so we collected our parcels and went up on deck. There was a swirling of water as the engine stopped and a dinghy, rowed with quick, excited strokes, came out to meet us. There was an exchange of Gaelic as we and the parcels were unloaded into the dinghy but though they were obviously glad to see us their greetings were at first a little strained. It was obvious that the family were much ashamed of having to admit that they had not laid in sufficient stocks of food to tide them over only three weeks' isolation. 'We've been spoiled with these vans comin',' they confessed after a glass or two of whisky from a bottle produced by Erchy had lessened the slight tension. 'We just let ourselves get slack but we'll see and not let it happen again.'

It developed into a very convivial ceilidh (whisky was the only form of sustenance our friends had not run short of) and by the time we came out again into the snow it was dark. I was faintly puzzled when I looked up at the full moon to discover that not only had it grown a waist but that it also seemed to have sprouted fuzzy whiskers. I realized with a fleeting sense of shame that the whisky had made me light-headed. Morag and Behag too showed signs of unusual elation and as soon as she had clambered aboard Morag went to lie down on one of the bunks, complaining of a 'frosted stomach'. I too eased myself down on to an unyielding lump of tarpaulin and stared with great contentment through half-shut eyes at that strangely shaped moon which was now wearing the porthole as a halo. The engine of the boat started; there was a rattle of chain as the anchor came aboard; 'goodbyes' were shouted. *Ealasaid* dipped gently as she was brought round and with the quickening of the engine the water thumped and swished against the stemhead. The fo'c'sle was full of a misty light and only an occasional sniff from Behag broke the steady pulsing of the engine and its accompanying clatter of enamel plates. It was with regret that I heard the home mooring being picked up and the engine switched off.

'I'm feelin' a change in the weather tonight,' said Erchy as we walked up from the shore.

'That's not what the forecasters are saying on the wireless,' I told him. 'They said only this morning that there was no sign of a break yet.'

'Ach, I don't care what the forecasters is sayin',' Erchy maintained. 'I can feel it kind of different an' your feelin's is a lot better than forecasts.'

'Aye,' agreed Hector soberly, 'an' tsey feel a lot furszer ahead.'

Two mornings later I awoke feeling that there was indeed a change. The light in my bedroom was sad and grey and there was the old familiar dripping of rain. Pulling back the curtains I saw that in the night the thaw had come leaving the moors as full of tracks as an upturned palm while the hills wept snowy tears. It rained relentlessly the whole of that day and the next day, which was a Sunday, the rain was accompanied by a truculent wind which came at us in great rushes that nearly caught us off balance as we trudged the sodden ground. Work done, I stayed snug in my cottage with a Howard Spring and a box of marshmallows for company and saw without contrition the good folk of the village trailing drably through the semi-dusk to church.

'I came to bring you this skart,' said Morag on Monday morning. 'Hector shot it on Saturday so you'll be able to cook it tomorrow.'

I thanked her and, taking the bird from her, hung it behind the kitchen door.

'An' do you know who lowered himself to come to our church last night?' she demanded with scarcely concealed amusement.

I shook my head.

'Well then, it was Euan! Him that's been sayin' ours is a dirty old church an' has been takin' to goin' to the other one at the far end of the village.'

'Good gracious!' I exclaimed. 'What's made him change back again, I wonder?'

'That's what I said to him just. "Euan," I asked him, "why are you not at your own church tonight when you've been sayin' it's so much better than ours an' that the missionary student fellow is such a good man?" An' do you know, Miss Peckwitt, he just blinked his eyes at me an he said: "What would I be doin' walkin' all that bloody way on a night like this? Is it daft you think I am?"'

VII. *The Nurse*

The nurse was extremely irate.

'What I don't do for these people here,' she complained loudly in a voice that sounded to me to be permanently pitched to a tone of grievance. 'And what thanks do I get for it? The way they treat me sometimes anybody would think I was trying to make them worse instead of better,' she elucidated with unwitting accuracy.

Our nurse was a fussy, prudish little woman with an occupational flush on her face and a halo of springy white curls that were only partly repressed by the severity of her dark blue felt hat. She must, when she was young, have been extremely pretty. She was still, if you took her feature by feature, a pretty woman but at fifty she had already achieved an appearance of senility by her splayed-foot walk, her habit of peering over the tops of her spectacles and by

143

the looseness of her pouting mouth.

I tipped the pail of shingle I had just carried up from the shore on to the path I was making and invited her inside for a 'strupak', the resentment I felt at having to leave off just when I was full of energy for my work being somewhat mitigated by the prospect of a couple of hours of indiscreet but very revealing gossip about my neighbours.

Though a Scot, the nurse was, like myself a 'foreigner' in Bruach and despite the fact that she had been residing among them for over twelve years she was not perceptibly nearer dispelling the prejudice of the crofters than she had been during her first twelve weeks. Undoubtedly for a stranger the task of nursing Bruachites was a difficult one— they could be testy enough on occasion—but so far as the crofters were concerned the nurse's chief disadvantage was that she did not speak their language: she 'hadn't the Gaelic'. If they became ill it might be too much of an effort to translate their needs into English, a complaint I felt was justified as it was obvious that however good their English they still thought in Gaelic and then effected the translation. Had the language difficulty been the only obstacle there is little doubt that time would have established a sufficiently cordial relationship, but time had elicited the fact that the nurse's shortcomings included an insatiable curiosity and an incorrigible tendency to gossip, so that despite her assiduous attentions when she was called in many of the Bruachites preferred to keep quiet about their ailments and to recover or die without her aid in either direction.

'Did you hear what Alistair Beag had the cheek to say

to me yesterday?' Nurse challenged me shrilly when she was seated.

I had heard, and like everyone else had been secretly delighted at its aptness but, turning my back to her while I filled the kettle, I professed ignorance.

'He told me I'd been here too long,' she declared, her voice brimming with outrage. 'In fact he shouted after me as I was leaving the house so that everybody could hear. "Away back to your bosses," he yelled at me. "Away back and tell them they should change the nurse here every three years the same as they do the bull!"' Her rather guileless blue eyes filled suddenly with tears and I felt a great pity for her. It was my impression that she had come to the village originally with the genuine aspiration to become a loved and respected figure—an Alma Mater to whom everyone would unhesitatingly turn in sickness or in trouble. The mixture of tolerance, pity and open antagonism that she had achieved must have been for her a bitter disappointment.

'I expect he was only saying it in fun,' I consoled. 'He says the most offensive things to me sometimes. It's just the sort of man he is.' I went on to tell her how a few days previously, having been particularly forgetful, I had been coming home from the village shop for the third time within a few hours when old Murdoch, who had been surveying the life of the community from the vantage point of his storm-damaged roof, had called out: 'Why, Miss Peckwitt! What are you at? You're here, there and everywhere today, just like the mavis.' Even while I was bestowing upon him a grin of fatuous appreciation the voice of Alistair Beag, who was hidden from me by the stone dyke he was rebuilding, had corroborated chummily, 'Aye, aye, she's been dodgin' about like a fart in a colander.'

The nurse appeared to be shocked. 'That's what I dislike so about them!' she exclaimed. 'They're so coarse! And they're immoral,' she went on. 'They blaspheme something terrible, and if they get near a pub they drink themselves silly. And then when the missionary comes round they sit there with their bibles on their knees and pretend they'd never think a dirty thought nor use a bad word. They're utter hypocrites!' She paused only while I refilled her cup. 'Of course,' she added, 'I see a lot more of what goes on than you do.'

'Of course,' I agreed.

'Hypocrites,' she repeated distastefully.

'Some of them aren't so bad,' I demurred.

'They're still hypocrites, even the best of them,' she insisted. 'Look at Anna there. She's what I'd call a really good woman. Yet you know she gets her water from the well out on the moor on Sundays instead of from Murdoch's croft right beside the road.'

I nodded. 'I know that,' I said.

'Well, isn't that sheer hypocrisy? She runs out of water but it's wicked to carry water on Sunday. So, sooner than let folks see her, she goes to the well out on the moor.'

I defended: 'But Anna does get extra water in from the well on a Saturday night. I see her regularly. And,' I went on, 'there are so many righteous people with nothing to do on a Sunday except just to pop into Anna's and have her give them tea. That's why she runs short of water.'

'Indeed it is,' agreed the nurse emphatically. 'But honestly, you'd think the Lord never knew a thing about what these folks do except what the missionary tells Him.' She took two or three quick sips at her tea and continued. 'You know Willy who I'm having to go and visit six and seven times a day? It's cancer, of course, and he's dying, as I daresay you know?'

I admitted that I knew, the village having diagnosed Willy's illness and assessed his probable expectation of life before the doctor had been called in, so that they were already speaking of him as though they were reading his obituary notice.

'Well, here's hypocrisy for you,' went on the nurse. 'Willy's in dreadful pain and there's no hope for him whatever but he's a Seceder and their religion doesn't allow the use of drugs. Every time I get near the door of that man's room his wife waylays me. "Now, Nurse," she says, "don't you be givin' him any of those drugs. We believe they're wicked." And then she leans over Willy. "Now, Willy," she says, "don't be askin' Nurse for drugs, you know you'll go to hell if you do." As soon as she's gone out of the room Willy turns to me with the tears and the sweat running off his face. "For God's sake, Nurse," he begs, "give me somethin' to stop the pain, I canna' bear it."'

'How awful,' I murmured. 'What do you do?'

'I give him a shot of morphia,' returned Nurse without hesitation. 'I'm not going to stand by and see a man suffer unnecessarily, religion or no religion.'

'Thank goodness!' I exclaimed. 'It would be awful to think of dear old Willy suffering like that.'

'His wife came in and caught me at it the other day—and nearly snatched the hypodermic from me.' She gave a dry little chuckle. 'She told me I was a vile and sinful woman bent on sending her husband to hell. I'd have laughed at her if I hadn't been so angry myself. Instead I told her to calm herself, it was only water I was giving him.'

'Do you think she believed you?' I asked incredulously.

'No, I don't think she did,' replied the nurse, 'but that's what they're like, these Seceders. They just want somebody else to take the responsibility of being the sinner.' She blew her nose to show she was feeling happier.

I said thoughtfully: 'There must be quite a lot of doctors and nurses who are Seceders. What happens then?'

She gave me a long knowing look from over her spectacles. 'I've worked for one,' she admitted. 'And never again, I hope. Of course, if their patients aren't Seceders they're doomed for hell anyway, so they get whatever drugs the doctor thinks they need. It's when the patient is a Seceder I don't like it.' She shuddered.

'They just let them suffer?' I prompted, hoping for her denial.

'Well, I'll tell you. Maybe you remember Ian Beg, who died not long after you'd come here? Now he was a Seceder, and so was the doctor we had at the time. When Ian was taken ill with cancer he said to the doctor, and I was there beside the bed at the time, "Now, Doctor," he said,

"I know I'm dying and I want you to promise me that no matter how much pain I'm in and how much I beg for relief you'll not prescribe drugs for me." The doctor warned him he would probably be in great pain, but Ian was adamant. So the doctor promised. Now I nursed that man till he died and there were times he nearly wrecked the bed in his agony and on a still night you could hear him moaning and crying with pain all over the village. It was terrible for his wife because she wasn't a Seceder. And it was terrible for me. I used to beg the doctor when he came to let me give Ian a shot of morphia but he wouldn't go back on his word. I've known me and Ian's wife to bury our heads in the hay in the barn to shut out the sound of his screaming when it was getting towards the end, and the hay would be wet with our tears after it.' She sighed a tired reminiscent sigh. 'Dear Lord, how that man suffered,' she said, 'but not one shot of anything did he have throughout his illness.'

She stared reflectively out of the window and for a few moments the kitchen was sad with our thoughts. 'Mind you,' she began again, 'there aren't many like Ian. Most of them are firm enough at denying others the use of drugs but when they get a wee twinge of pain themselves they're soon after me to do something about it.'

While we had been talking the still water of the bay had become progressively shadowed and I could hear my hens questioning the delay of their evening feed. I asked the nurse to excuse me while I attended to them. She looked at the clock. 'I suppose I ought to be going, really,' she said with obvious reluctance, 'but I'm enjoying my wee ceilidh, and I've got to go and see to Willy again in an hour's time. It doesn't seem worth going home in the meantime.'

I suggested she should stay.

'Well, I'll need to use your toilet,' she said. 'That is if you've got one.'

'Of course,' I said, a little indignant.

'There's no "of course" about it,' she retorted. 'I had a friend of mine staying with me last year and I left her in one of the houses while I was attending to a patient. She'd been drinking a lot of tea of course and when she got uncomfortable she asked if she could use their toilet. The woman looked at her and said straight out, "I'm afraid we haven't one." My friend was a bit put out and I suppose she couldn't help showing it. "You haven't one?" she gasped. The old woman gave her a haughty look and said, "No, we never felt the need of one yet." Of course that made my friend think they'd only just moved into the house so she said, "Oh, I see, you haven't been here long, then?" "Why, yes indeed," the old woman replied. "We've been here twenty-five years." I just got back into the kitchen then and saw the look on my friend's face. We got out of the house and she turned to me. "Nurse," she said, "that old woman's just told me they've lived here for twenty-five years and they've never needed a lavatory. Aren't they peculiar?"' Nurse laughed. 'I had to hurry up and explain that their peculiarity wasn't biological, it was just that they always used the calf shed.'

'It amuses me the way they just cut a hole in the front and back of the little boys' pants so that they don't need to use nappies or train them to pot,' I said. 'It's certainly very effective.'

'Sheer bone-idle laziness!' snorted the nurse, who had water laid on in her own house and so was not burdened with the task of carrying every drop needed for washing.

I showed her my 'wee hoosie' as I rushed off to feed the hens and put out hay, praying that Bonny would be waiting at the moor gate when Erchy went to let in his own cows, so that she would come home alone without my having to go looking for her in the dark after the nurse had gone.

'My goodness!' said Nurse admiringly when I came back into the kitchen. 'You're quite civilized with your toilet.'

I laughed. 'It seems a bit barbaric to me still.'

The problem of sewage disposal in Bruach was, as it must be in every sewerless and waterless village, a difficult and distasteful business. Chemical lavatories are not the answer, certainly where there is no man available for emptying them. They are too heavy for a woman to lift when they are even half full and somewhat wasteful of time and chemical if they are emptied more frequently. I had solved the sewage problem by having two adjoining lavatories; an ordinary chemical one for serious visits and an invention of my own for the more flippant occasions. The idea had come when I had started keeping a cow and found that though she was put into her byre sometimes about four o'clock in an afternoon and not let out again until ten o'clock the following morning the shingle bottom of the trench behind her was always completely dry. At first I had thought of calling in the vet but after being adequately reassured by Bonny herself I realized that from the byre the land sloped down to the shore so evidently her urine just ran into the shingle and seeped its way into the sea. I worked on this principle for my second lavatory. First I dug a hole in the shingle floor of my 'wee hoosie' and into the hole I lowered a section of chimney lining that I had begged from old Murdoch. An old galvanized pan with holes punched roughly in its bottom sat in the chimney lining and this was then topped with a substantial box seat. In the 'wee hoosie' I also kept a pail of sea water so that it could be 'flushed' immediately after use. It was a simple arrangement but it worked beautifully, and I use the adverb deliberately for on nights when the sea water was full of 'noctiluca', those minute organisms which give the sea its phosphorescence, I have waited entranced until the last of the scintillating water has gurgled down from the pail, leaving it transformed by a luminous coating that still glowed greenly as I shut the door.

'I'll be coming here more often now that I know you've a nice little place like that,' threatened the nurse. 'I usually have to wait until I get to Janet's up the road there. She lets me use the toilet they have for the tourists in summer,' she explained. 'But you know, Miss Beckwith,' she continued, 'that's where you have it with these people. They've gone to the trouble of building a "wee hoosie" so that the tourists have somewhere to go and they even keep a toilet roll in it. But they have the toilet roll fixed to the ceiling instead of the wall.'

'That's a funny place for it,' I commented.

'Isn't it?' agreed the nurse. 'I said to her: "Janet," I said, "why on earth do you keep the toilet roll up on the ceiling? It's awful hard for a wee body like myself to reach up there when I want it." "Well, Nurse," she told me, "it's like this. Shamus keeps his pet sheep in there at night and if I don't have the toilet roll way up out of its reach the beast has eaten the lot by morning."

'If they have a shed it mustn't be wasted,' I observed with a smile; 'and really I suppose it's understandable. A "wee hoosie" is only a status symbol that their children insist on when they come home from university. You'll notice that a house where there are no young folk doesn't usually have even the crudest of privies. The old folk seem to find it unnatural to shut themselves up in a confined space to relieve themselves.'

'Yes.' The nurse nodded vigorously. 'But when they're getting older and they don't want to face the storms, that's when the trouble begins. Then it's "Nurse, Nurse, I haven't cacced for days, will ye give me a dose?" You'd wonder too at the amount of calomel it takes to shift them.' She sighed. 'Oh, well, I suppose I must go and give Willy his injection—' She broke off. 'Goodness, I've just remembered I'd promised the teacher I'd go down and inspect the children's heads today. She's been complaining about them.'

I looked at her without speaking.

'They were in a shocking state when I attended to them before.'

'How do they get them?' I asked. 'Most of the houses seem to be pretty clean.'

'It's just the one or two that aren't that cause the trouble,' she said. 'I always have to undress on a sheet when I've been anywhere near them.' She moved a few steps towards the door, still loath to say good night. 'Dear knows what time I'll get home tonight,' she said with her hand on the latch. 'I have to go and see Barabal yet. I suppose you've heard about Barabal?'

'No!' I said with some surprise. 'Is she ill?'

'No,' replied the nurse with a look that was meant to convey something out of the ordinary. 'She's not ill but the doctor went to see her last week.'

'But why did the doctor go to see her if she's not ill?' I felt foolish the moment the question was off my lips.

'Well, I mustn't say in my position, must I? But you'd think she'd have had more sense at her age.' The nurse's mouth collapsed into a droop of disapproval but her eyes regarded me eagerly from above the spectacles.

'Well, I never!' I said, lapping it all up without a qualm of conscience. 'Is Barabal married?'

'Not at all.' The nurse's tone implied that no man would have been fool enough to marry Barabal.

'Who's the father supposed to be, then?' I asked, overcome with curiosity.

'Nobody here anyway. They say she went to Glasgow for it.' The nurse was still contemptuous. 'She was there for a couple of months in the summer, anyway.' She opened the door and stepped out into a drizzle of dusky rain. 'I wish I'd remembered about Barabal being Alistair Beag's sister when he was shouting insults at me the other day,'

she said. 'I could have told him if anyone had been anywhere too long it was his sister in Glasgow.' She got halfway down the path and I stood in the doorway watching
her. 'Change the nurse like they change the bull, indeed,'
she was muttering as she went out through the gate. 'I wish
I'd remembered it.'

VIII. *Kirsty*

'ACH, THAT WOMAN!' commented Morag.

I had just told her that I was on my way to visit Kirsty, Johnny Comic's sister, to see if she would sell me a bag of potatoes.

'Aye,' went on Morag, 'I doubt she'll sell you a bag, though she'd have but one left to do herself. Let her see your money an' she'll not be able to say no to you.'

Morag was standing in the doorway of her cottage, bending over a rubbing-board which stood in a zinc bath of soapy water. The washed clothes she had flung aside into another tin bath which stood outside catching the wind-harried douche of water from a piece of leaky guttering, for it was still raining torrentially. (In Bruach where there was no piped water we washed on wet days and, if it was calm enough, optimistically hung out the washing on the

157

line to wait for the dry day that would come. With this treatment—sometimes hours, sometimes days, of crystal clear rain coursing through them—our clothes needed no artificial bleaches to get that 'extra whiteness'.)

'You do dislike Kirsty, don't you?' I said. Morag looked shocked.

'Ach, it's no' that I mislike her at all. It's just the way of her.'

'What way?' I asked.

'Well, mo ghaoil, I'm tellin' you, she's that grand seemin' an' whenever any of us women hereabouts that's been in service go to speak to her we always get the feelin' that the first thing she's goin' to say to us is, "And can you do a little flannel washing, my dear?"' She stretched her neck and screwed up her lips to convey the condescension of a duchess and looked at me to see if I understood. 'It's what the mistresses always used to ask when I was girl in service,' she supplied by way of explanation.

'Was Kirsty never in service herself?' I asked.

'No, indeed, she was not. Not service as we knew it, anyway. All my fine Kirsty did was to push one of them rich invalid ladies around in a wheelbarrow.' She tossed her head haughtily. Drawing aside the bath so that I could step round it, she resumed, 'I saw you comin' so I called to Erchy to pour out a cup of tea for you.' Erchy was sitting on the bench under the window with his elbows resting on the back of it. He had taken off his oilskins but his cap was still on his head, pushed well back so that it would not drip over his face. With a limp gesture of acknowledgement he indicated that the cup of tea beside him on the bench was for me.

Opposite Erchy and within convenient spitting distance of the fire sat Neilly Ally, an old uncle of Morag's, who had arrived unheralded on the bus one evening, as crofters' relatives appeared to have a habit of doing, and who had been in semi-residence with her ever since. He took his pipe out of his mouth briefly to say 'Aye' by way of greeting. Although Neilly had lived in Glasgow for over fifty years he had not shed the aura of the croft and, sitting there with his disordered white hair, his blue seaman's jersey and his dark crumpled trousers he looked as though he might just have come in from the shore after hauling his boat. There was a bowl of soapy water on the floor beside him—another acknowledgement of the bounteous rain—and his newly washed feet resting on the slab of driftwood that did duty as a kerb looked as though they had been more accustomed to paddling in peaty burns than treading Glasgow's pavements. In the intervals of puffing his pipe and spitting uninhibitedly he was engaged in scraping the tar off a netting needle, a task which appeared to require a disproportionate amount of concentration.

'Well,' said Erchy, rousing himself, 'are you pleased with the weather?'

'I am not,' I replied. 'I'm tired of this rain, rain, rain, day after day. I can't get anything done.'

Neilly Ally ceased his scraping momentarily. ''Tis no' as bad as in the Bible when it rained forty days and forty nights,' he soothed.

'How do you know? You weren't there,' said Erchy pertly.

The old man stared aloofly through the window above Erchy's head. 'Was I no', then?' he enquired in a tone that implied there could be some doubt about it, and glancing again at his white spongy-looking feet I almost believed there might be.

Morag came in, wiping her hands on the edges of her coat. 'You're not sittin' down, Miss Peckwitt,' she chided me.

'Not as wet as I am,' I told her. 'I'm more comfortable standing.'

She picked up the teapot and tilting it drained the remains of the tea into her own cup.

'This weather,' she grumbled. 'You'd think the sky would have got tired of flingin' the rain at us the way it's been doin'. I don't remember weather like this when I was a girl. Wind we had, but not all this rain.'

'They say the bombs has changed it all,' put in Erchy, 'but ach, I don't believe it's that at all.'

Neilly, who had been sitting in an offended silence since Erchy's previous remark, now sat up. With great deliberation he put the netting needle on the table and placed his pipe beside it.

''Tis no' the bombs,' he pronounced, fixing us with an impressive blue gaze. 'It started before the bombs, I can tell you.'

'Aye?' encouraged Erchy.

'I'm tellin' you, what spoiled the weather altogether was when that ship the *Titanic* hit that iceberg. The weather's never been the same since that day.' He fitted his pipe back between his lips and took up his netting needle again, indifferent to our varied expressions.

'Aye?' murmured Erchy politely.

'Aye?' repeated Morag curiously.

'Aye?' I echoed faintly.

Erchy changed the subject. 'Did I hear you sayin' you was goin to Tornish?' His voice was only faintly interrogative.

'Yes, I'm going to call on Kirsty.'

'Ach, that woman!' spluttered Erchy through a mouthful of tea.

It was always the same whenever anyone mentioned the name of Kirsty. 'Ach, that woman!' would be the rejoinder. The tone might be disparaging, combative, outraged or contemptuous but the phrase prefaced any further comment no matter how her name cropped up in the conversation, and it amused me that the woman should appear to go out of her way to get herself so much disliked.

Sooner or later Kirsty mortally offended everyone with whom she came into contact and yet the strange thing was that she was never ostracized. It would be safe to say, I think, that she was completely unloved but never hated. The women disliked her intensely during the few minutes' altercation she permitted herself to have with them from time to time and from which she always emerged victorious. The men detested her temporarily and mumbled epithets for a few days after she had humiliated them, which she did with great deliberation but without apparent malice. But her acid comments on neighbours were too much relished for enlivening the ceilidhs for there to be any risk of her being ignored for long and her reputation for always providing a 'good dram' for any man who did an odd job for her ensured that she was well looked after.

A rigid Presbyterian, she had been known to refuse point blank a lift from church in a visitor's car one stormy Sabbath with the words: 'Some may not care what becomes of their souls but others know what is right from what is wrong.' And when the much discomfited minister had put his head out of the window of the car and assured Kirsty that it was no sin—'Wasn't he himself taking the chance of it?'—she had shrivelled him back into his seat with the retort, 'Maybe it is no sin for you, but I'm takin' no risks with my soul.' The rest of the congregation still within earshot had been quietly outraged. As they said afterwards, 'Wasn't it a wild wet night anyway for such a walk an' after all wasn't the minister himself only gettin' a lift to Kirsty's own house where he always lodged on a Sunday night because there was no bus back to his village until the Monday morning, poor man.' I have often wondered which of them asked the blessing on the cold supper they would have shared that night.

Erchy stood up. 'Ach, if you're goin' that way I suppose I might just as well come with you,' he volunteered, setting his cap with the peak at the back in deference to the wild weather. 'I was thinkin' it was time I went to see Dugan about some rams an' it's on my way.'

'See and take care Kirsty doesn't get a hold of you,' Morag called out to him insinuatingly as we started off.

'Hell, no!' returned Erchy. He bestowed upon me what from someone less unsophisticated might have been a leer but from him was only a crumpled smile.

'You heard about that?' he asked me.

'No,' I said, 'tell me.'

'Well, I'd just done a bit of cementin' for her. That bit of path you mind, down by her shed. When I'd finished she had my strupak ready an' we had a wee ceilidh an' then she poured me out a good dram. She didn't take one herself an' I was sittin' by the fire drinkin' mine down an' feelin' good inside when she said all of a sudden, "Erchy, did I ever tell you about the time I saw a naked man?" God! I near dropped the glass out of my hand I was that scared, an' I was sweatin' that much I thought the drops would run down an' spoil my whisky.' (I should perhaps mention that in Gaeldom there is no age at which a woman ceases to be regarded as a seductress.) 'Then she went on tellin' me that when she was a girl she was standin' on the shore an' she saw a man come out of the water an' walk up the beach an' he had nothin' on at all! She ran all the way home an' told her mother an' all her mother did was to give her a good thrashin' for not shuttin' her eyes. I can tell you,' said Erchy with a grunt, 'I finished my whisky an' grabbed my coat an' was off out of the house as fast as I could go, an' that old cailleach just stood in the door an' watched me an' she was laughin' that funny way she has, you know? Indeed, I believe she did it on purpose, just to see me sweat.'

We picked our way through the rivulet that was normally a dry sheep-track to the open moor where the wind, still full of the smell of tangle, doubled its strength, threatening to tear the buttons off our oilskins, whipping our clothes against our legs and rattling the rain against our sou'westers, so that all other sound than the plodding of our boots was shut out. With chins tucked resolutely down into our coat collars and gloved hands hooked into pockets (the latter filled with rain too easily to plunge our hands deep into them) we battled to the comparative shelter of the glen where the track was less exacting and I was able to forge ahead of Erchy. Although I never found the prospect of walking the moors in a storm remotely inviting there was at times, I confess, something almost pleasantly hypnotic about it once I had accepted the necessity for my journey and was well and truly embarked upon it. Shut inside oilskins and sou'wester and hearing nothing but the rain, one has the feeling of being insulated not only from the weather but from the world in general. Because superfluous movement would expose chinks in the carefully disposed insulation one limits one's gaze to the path immediately in front of one's feet. In any case there is no perceptible movement to distract one's eye. The ubiquitous rabbits, the busy shrews, the sinuous stoats, are all snug in their secret places. The cattle and sheep, having found a sheltered corrie, lie there, patiently cudding. There are no trees on the moors to be lashed into dervish dances; no tatters of bracken whirling on the wind. Everything that is not securely anchored has been wrested away in the first few hours of the storm. So, one plods on tranquilly, building and rebuilding a lifetime of dreams while one's feet seem to stride without conscious effort over the stiff black heather roots and the flayed grass, so abject in its surrender.

'Hi!'

I halted guiltily as I heard Erchy's shout, for I had forgotten all about him.

'My,' he grumbled as he panted up to me. 'You're a fast woman.'

I smiled at him.

'Aye, you can laugh, but folks shouldn't rush like that over these moors. You'll get heart trouble or somethin'. That's why people here live so long, you know. It's because they never hurry.' His face was peony red with exertion and polished by the rain.

Realizing that I too was breathless, I slowed my pace and so it was nearly half an hour later than I had reckoned before we started to come down the hill and could see the stone dykes and croft houses of the village.

'Kirsty's croft isn't a very big one, is it?' I asked Erchy, for now we were in the shelter of the hill and could converse without too much effort

'Ach, she's no' needin' a very big one. She only keeps the one cow anyway an' if she thinks her hay's a wee bit short she just helps herself to what's on other people's crofts.'

'No!' I protested.

'Aye, she does indeed. My uncle used to have the croft next to her but he gave it up because of her. When he'd go to cut his hay he'd find Kirsty had cut that much of it over his boundary—an' the best of it, too.'

'But he could have stopped her, surely?'

'You cannot stop that woman doin' anythin' she's set her mind to,' said Erchy. 'When he spoke to her about it she just reared herself up the way she does an' told him she'd cut hay wherever she wanted. "But that's my own croft I pay rent for," my uncle told her, "an' that grass you've cut was growin' on my own land." "Indeed," Kirsty says to him, "supposin' it was growin' on your own chin, I'd still cut it." My uncle was that mad about it but there was nothin' he could do except complain to the Land Court an' they wouldn't have been able to stop her from doin' it. They would only have told her not to.'

We came in sight of Kirsty's cottage, easily identifiable by its piebald appearance. Johnny had been directed to cement-wash it during the summer and had almost completed the task when he had discovered a large and beautiful spider's web suspended from the guttering. Unable to bring himself to destroy it he had left that part of the wall uncemented and by the time Kirsty had returned to coerce him the rain had started and it had been raining off and on ever since.

'Poor Johnny Comic,' I said, for in contrast to the excessive gentleness of Johnny's nature Kirsty was rock hard. She had been twelve years old when her brother was born and, perhaps because her mother had never fully recovered after the event and had died less than a year later, it seemed as if she had never forgiven him for the presumptuousness of being born at all. Six years later their father had died and Kirsty at eighteen had been left to cope alone with the infant Johnny. People said that from that time she seemed to have become obsessed with the idea of thwarting his every wish, and though she had fed him adequately, clothed him and kept him clean, his presence in the house had irritated her and thus Johnny's wanderings had begun at an early age. When he returned home he was given his porridge and boiled egg meal and unrelentingly sent to bed, no matter if it was only six o'clock in the evening. He had been so repressed that even when he was a grown man he was too docile to protest at the arrangement and so it had continued for nearly sixty years. He was allowed no money of his own although Kirsty's income, thanks to a small annuity left to her by the 'lady in the wheelbarrow', was more than adequate for their standard of living. The only indulgence she permitted her brother was a grudging access to the tin of baking-soda in her cupboard, and even this small comfort was hidden away if she considered his consumption excessive.

'You'd think she'd let Johnny keep a pet of some sort,' Erchy said. 'It wouldn't do her any harm an' it would be good for Johnny.'

'Someone did give him a baby rabbit a little while ago,' I said. 'Wasn't he allowed to keep that?'

'No, indeed. Kirsty killed it as soon as she could get a hold of it.'

'She's a real bitch!' I said feelingly, recalling the rapt expression on Johnny's face when he was fondling a cat or a dog and his anguish when he found an injured bird.

'Look at the way she was last year with that bird's nest,'

continued Erchy. 'While she was away seein' her cousin last spring the birds built a nest in the chimney of "the room". Johnny was up to it every day on a ladder watchin' it. When the birds was just about ready to fly Kirsty came home an' sees it, an' though I believe Johnny went down on his knees pleadin' with her to wait only a couple of days for them to leave the nest Kirsty just took paper an' paraffin an' lit a roarin' fire in the grate an' roasted the poor wee things to death.'

We opened the gate to the grassy plot that Kirsty kept trimmed so expertly by means of a hay scythe and she herself appeared on the doorstep. Her face expressed surprise but I suspected she had seen us coming. She had in her hand a barometer which she held up in the rain.

'Look at that!' she addressed it crossly as we came within earshot. 'Take a good look at it, will you, an' then dare to tell me it's fair weather!' Giving it an admonitory shake before hooking it savagely back on the wall in the porch she turned to us. 'That thing has a face full of lies,' she said.

Erchy turned and winked at me, while Kirsty, satisfied she had given him a good story for the next ceilidh, bade us take off our dripping oilskins and 'come away inside'.

The kitchen into which she led us was blatant in its discomfort. The wooden walls were painted a shiny gasometer green and were completely unrelieved by pictures or hangings of any sort except for an embroidered cloth bag which bulged with mail-order catalogues. These, with the Bible and hymn-book prominent on the windowsill, were the only literature Kirsty permitted herself. The linoleum too was shiny and green and sketchily patterned with small dark circles that reminded me of the eyes of a moribund sheep. The table was covered with American cloth, white and new-looking; the big black range gleamed with polish; the cushionless wooden chairs and the bench shone with many coats of varnish. The whole place looked almost sterile in its cleanliness and about as comfortless and uninviting as a fishmonger's empty slab.

Kirsty swung the big kettle over the huddle of peats which were smouldering apologetically in the grate. She next dipped some pieces of driftwood into a can of paraffin that stood in a corner of the room and then poked them carefully between the peats. Bending down she blew with big capable breaths, quickly coaxing them into flame. The kettle began to send forth a subdued spout of steam.

'I'm sayin' the peats didn't get properly dry at all this year, the weather's been that bad,' Kirsty said.

Erchy and I looked at each other understandingly. We knew that she claimed more peat hags, cut more peats and yet used fewer than anyone else in the village. We knew that the big shed at the back of the house was bulging with dry peats left over from the previous year's cutting and that the complaint of wet peats was only an excuse for the meagreness of the fire.

She set out one of her best cups for me and an old chipped one for Erchy. Let it be said that neither he nor I felt we could manage another strupak coming so soon after the one we had taken with Morag but we sat and meekly watched Kirsty brewing tea and buttering oatcakes without so much as a whisper of protest from either of us. She poured out a cup of tea for herself but as it was an inflexible rule with her never to eat or drink anything while there was still steam coming from it she took up some crochet work and talked to us with condescending affability while we sipped and ate. She appeared to do a great deal of crocheting although there was no evidence of a finished article to break the austerity of the room. I wondered how she disposed of it as I watched her large male-looking hands weaving the fine threads into intricate patterns of scrolls and scallops with enviable dexterity.

Kirsty was an impressive woman, now in her seventies yet still standing nearly six foot tall. Like her brother she had a pale, fine skin and very large hands but there any resemblance between them ended. Kirsty's pale grey eyes could have been put in by a glazier. Her mouth was like a tight-drawn thread. Her black hair which one felt had never had the temerity to turn grey seemed only to have rusted at the ends and was clamped to her head, pancake fashion, and stuck with so many pins it made one think of an ancient cow-pat that the starlings had been foraging in. She was dressed, as always, in black relieved only by a chit of white at the throat on which a jet brooch was pinned with geometric care, and it was this slight adornment, I think, as much as anything else that underlined her appearance of hauteur and made it easy to understand Morag's reference to 'flannel-washing'.

I was about to broach the subject of potatoes when

Kirsty gave a faint exclamation of impatience and withdrawing the crochet hook from her work she pushed it between her lips.

'Miss Peckwitt,' she said, 'I have what is like a soreness in my teeths here. I believe it must be what they call "the toothache".'

I was a shade surprised to hear Kirsty admit to any physical discomfort and was temporarily at a loss for words.

Erchy came to the rescue. 'You'll need to go to the doctor and get it sorted,' he told her.

'Indeed I will not then,' she replied with asperity.

'It'll be much better to get it seen to,' I murmured. 'The doctor will surely see to it as you're so far from a dentist.'

Kirsty crocheted industriously for a few moments and then she said: 'The last time I went to the doctor I was twelve or thereabouts. I'd cut my thumb near off on the scythe, for we'd been cuttin' the corn. Look at that, now!' She showed us the distorted thumb on her right hand. 'It was hangin' right back against my hand, if you can believe it,' she continued, 'and my father said I was to go and see the doctor with it. He walked with me himself to the surgery and that's near fourteen miles, and there I had it put back on and stitched into place. The doctor gave me nothin' to help the pain and he said I was so quiet about it he'd give me a sweetie to suck to help pass the time while I was walkin' back home. It was one of them big sweeties, I forget what you call them, but I mind I didn't feel like eatin' it until I got nearly home again. When I did put it into my mouth and bit it, it was that hard I broke two of my teeths on it and my mouth started to bleed like I would bleed to death. My father just turned me round and walked me all the way back to the doctor's again. I've never been near their kind since.'

At that moment there was a stamping of feet in the porch and Johnny Comic came into the kitchen. He had obviously tramped a long way home and the rain was dripping from his cap and running from his oilskin wrappers. He greeted us offhandedly and went straight to the dresser, took down a cup and taking it over to the fire lifted the teapot which Kirsty had refilled with water from the kettle.

'Where's the cow?' Kirsty asked, fixing him with a glacial stare.

'She's at the moor gate,' Johnny replied, pouring tea that was like singed water into his cup.

'Then away and get her,' commanded Kirsty imperiously.

'I'll take this drink first, I'm thirsty,' said Johnny with a bravado that we knew was buttressed by our presence.

'You'll away and get her,' repeated Kirsty. Her expression did not change, her fingers did not falter over her crocheting but her voice had an undertone that apparently was not lost on Johnny. He put down the teapot obediently, took his stick and was about to go through the door when Kirsty called him back.

'You'll not be needin' your stick,' she told him.

'But the bull's there with her,' Johnny began pleadingly. 'I'll never get her away from him without a stick.'

'You'll leave your stick,' repeated Kirsty.

Johnny's face crumpled but he left the stick by the door and shambled out. 'If he takes the stick I cannot trust him not to lay it across the cow,' she explained.

Erchy and I exchanged glances. It was ridiculous for her to suggest that gentle old Johnny would beat an animal. We knew and Kirsty knew that he wanted the stick only for brandishing in front of the bull if the animal was determined to follow, for he was timid where the larger animals were concerned. But there revealed was Kirsty's one weakness. Her cow. It and it only had found the one flaw in her petrified emotions. It was an odd beast of nondescript breed, swag-bellied, small-hoofed, and with horns that looked like malignant growths but she had reared it from a calf and she still lavished upon it all the care and affection that less eccentric natures would have bestowed upon an only child. She was constantly feeding it tit-bits from the house and it ate them all. Biscuits, chocolate, cake, cheese, bread and jam. 'Ach, it's no' a right beast at all to eat them things,' people were apt to comment. It did seem, even to a tyro like myself, that the cow was unnatural and many times when I had passed the cottage I had paused in wonder when I saw its great behind sticking out of the doorway, only the narrowness of the entrance and the width of its belly seeming to prevent it from pushing its way into the spruce kitchen.

So far as Kirsty was concerned the cow could do no wrong. So far as Johnny was concerned it could do no right. If Johnny had been capable of hating anything at all he would have hated that cow. As it was he merely accepted philosophically its domination of the household. He had to cut hay for it, he had to carry water for it, he had to muck out its byre and drive it to and from the moor when Kirsty did not fancy the weather and he did it all uncomplainingly and under a constant barrage of sarcasm from his sister. The only times Johnny became exasperated were when the cow broke into his beloved flower garden. In Bruach, where gardens were invariably feeding grounds for poultry or bone-chewing sanctuaries for the dogs, Johnny's love of flowers was considered to be just another of his queernesses. It was quite understandable that Kirsty should have a garden, surrounded by a barricade impenetrable even for a cow, where she grew excellent vegetables for sale to the summer tourists, but Johnny's anthomania they found incomprehensible. It was a pity that the only land he was allowed to have for his hobby was a small plot at the windward side of the house where a few sad blackcurrant bushes brooded over the mouldering stones of a derelict shed. Laboriously he had dug out enough stones to give him a little soil in which to transplant wild primroses from the moors or seeds and plants he begged from the Laird's gardener; but as soon as the plants grew into a green and tasty mouthful Kirsty's cow would come and with calculating greed work at his shaky stone dyke until she could break in and devour the lot. Every year Johnny tried, indifferent to his sister's upbraidings for wasting his time. Every year the cow outwitted him. Not having any money to buy fencing he would scrounge old pieces of wire netting wherever he could and carry shafts of driftwood of formidable size for miles from the shore to reinforce the dyke, but he never once succeeded in keeping out the cow until the flowers came into bloom.

There was a bellow from outside of a cow demanding attention. Kirsty put down her crochet. Erchy and I got up and started to put on our oilskins. I mentioned the subject of potatoes. She could, it seemed, let me have a bag to see me on. Much relieved, I took out my purse.

'Are you wantin' them in a hurry?' she asked.

'Well, yes,' I admitted. 'I've only enough for a couple of days at the most, and I haven't much else in the way of vegetables either. I wish I knew your secret of getting vegetables to grow,' I told her.

'They're too damty scared not to,' whispered Erchy in a languid aside.

I really was envious of Kirsty's garden for in return for all the attention I bestowed on mine it yielded little more than a few weary lettuce, half-hearted cabbage and wind-shrivelled beans while hers seemed to produce near prize-winning specimens with Kirsty doing little else but act as overseer.

Her thread of a mouth tautened into the vestige of a superior smile. She more than anyone else had always despised me as too weak and incompetent to tackle the crofting life and doubtless my admission confirmed her opinion.

'You'll get your potatoes tomorrow, then,' she promised, and then as we were leaving she said with sudden cordiality, 'You should come and ceilidh with me more often.'

'I would,' I told her with shocking insincerity, 'but it's

such a long tramp over the hill.' I was conscious of a whimsical look from the corner of Erchy's eye.

''Tis nothin' at all,' she scoffed. And as if to prove her statement she arrived at my cottage the very next day with a hundredweight of potatoes strapped to her back. She had carried them all the way over the hill track because she had promised I should have them and the carrier's lorry had broken down.

IX. *The Green Halo*

IT WAS A RIPE, RED BERRY of an autumn day, bloomed with haze and tinged with sunshine and I was busy in my kitchen making jam from brambles which had grown fat and taste-less from the superabundance of summer rain.

'Here, did you hear the news?' demanded Erchy, standing in the doorway and swinging in his hand a large hammer with which he was expecting to do some repairs to Bonny's byre.

'About Peggy?' I asked, for all the village had been laughing yesterday because poor Peggy, who was known to be over ninety and who still worked all the hours God sends, had waylaid the doctor when he was visiting in the village and asked him why she should have become so bent. She never used to be, she told him ingenuously.

'No, indeed. Not about Peggy at all but about Johnny Comic's accident?'

'No!' I said, immediately serious. 'What's happened?'

'He was knocked down by a lorry on the road yesterday an' they've taken him off to hospital.'

'Was he much hurt?' I asked him.

'The nurse didn't seem to think so,' Erchy supplied. 'But they won't know for a day or two till they get the X-rays.' He stayed in the doorway, his sturdy peasant body enclosed by the sunlight. 'Come an' tell me what I'm to do,' he ordered.

'I can't leave this at the moment,' I said, glancing anxiously at the full pan which was bubbling to within half an inch of the rim.

He came over and stood beside the stove.

'You haven't much freeboard there,' he commented. 'I only hope it'll keep calm for you.'

'If, instead of being clever, you would go and look inside the byre you'll see for yourself what needs doing,' I told him with mock severity as I carefully slid the preserving pan away from the heat. He left me to my task and when the jam had achieved a 'jell' I poured it into jars, labelled them and put them in the larder and then stood back to admire. I derive more pleasure from a well-stocked larder than from a well-stocked wardrobe, particularly if the shelves are packed with the result of my own labours, but in Bruach I was denied the satisfaction of attaining a really adequate supply of preserves because there was too much wind for fruit growing and rather more than most vegetables can stand. As a consequence they were always scarce and expensive and so it was a matter of making use of the more despised representatives of the earth's bounty. Elderberries I had already made into jelly and wine and this year the blaeberries which hid themselves in squat leafy clumps in sheltered parts of the moor had been so plentiful that even after the children had sated themselves on them the smell of the neglected berries fermenting in the moss had come to us on a wine-scented breeze. For the brambles I had searched the freckled moors diligently, finding the bushes squandering themselves over and into abandoned peat-hags. Now I awaited the fast-ripening rowanberries, and hoped to outwit the starlings which each evening gathered in the tree behind the house and smacked their beaks over the feast that was to come.

Morag and the fat and jovial Anna Vic, each with a creel of peats on her back, went past the cottage as I was carrying the preserving pan outside to fill it with rainwater from the tank.

'Put those down a minute and come and have a wee strupak,' I called. 'I'm just going to make one.'

They lowered their creels on to the stone dyke and came through the gate. 'My, but your garden is beautiful just,' Anna Vic observed, and added, 'You English are the great ones for your flowers right enough.'

My garden was certainly looking its best now that a spell of calm weather had at last allowed the flowers to bloom unmolested and, though the winds had shrivelled some plants beyond resuscitation and delay had paled the vividness the rest would have revealed had they managed to flower earlier, they nevertheless made an attractive display. There was variety in the colour of the late lupins and in the gold and yellows of the calendulas while large clumps of honesty held out their flat pods to be silvered by the sunshine. The lupins had been sent to me from England. The seeds of the calendulas and honesty too had been purchased from an English firm and yet, though they may be exactly the same variety and from the same nursery, the flowers in a Hebridean garden never seem to achieve the poise and glamour of the flowers in an English garden. Their stems grow stockier, perhaps because of their continual struggle with the storms. The blooms are always either wind harried or rain stressed but when they do burst into flower there is about them a buoyancy and virility which suggest that they too might have shed some of the constraint of English life.

My two friends sat down and when I had brewed tea I called Erchy to come in for a cup. With him came Donald Beag who had, surprisingly, mislaid the hook that did duty for one of his arms and who had been on his way to the shore where he thought he might have left it.

Erchy was glancing ruefully down at the bottom of his trouser leg which he had caught on a nail in the byre and torn. He asked whether there were any tinkers in the vicinity from whom he might get a new pair.

'There was one in the village yesterday,' Anna Vic told him. 'But he had nothin' but things for the children except for some nighties.' Her voice became shrill. 'He was wantin' me to buy a nightie from him. "I don't want a nightie," I told him. But ah, he kept on at me, "Buy a nightie from me, mistress." "I don't want another nightie," I said, "my drawers is stuffed with nighties."'

'Is that what it is?' interpolated Erchy with a mischievous glance at her well-padded hips. 'Well, all I can say is, it's a damty funny place to keep your nighties.'

'You wretch!' Anna Vic flung at him, hovering between amusement and vexation.

'I'll bet you bought a nightie from him all the same,' I challenged her, for her heart was pure gold.

'Ach, well, you don't like to send them away without takin' anythin' from them an' it was no use me buyin' children's clothes.'

'I wish I could hear of the same tink as I got this pair from,' said Erchy, looking down at his torn trousers again. 'Maybe he doesn't look much good now but he was a good trouser when he was new.'

The talk soon switched to Johnny Comic's accident.

'However did he come to be knocked down by a lorry?' said I, thinking of the deserted Bruach road which saw a lorry about three or four times a week at its busiest.

'Ach, the driver says he wasn't there one minute an' the next he's just down in front of the wheel. He thinks Johnny was standin' up on the dyke beside the road there an' either a bit of the dyke slipped or Johnny just tripped an' fell down,' said Morag.

'It's a bad business, anyway,' said Donald. 'An old man like that havin' to go to hospital.'

'The nurse said she didn't think anythin' was broken,' Morag assured us.

'If he's nothin' broken yet then they'll break somethin' for him in hospital,' said Donald, with conviction. 'They'll not have him in there with nothin' wrong with him.'

'Ach, likely they'll give him a dose of castor oil an' send him home in a day or two,' said Erchy. 'I believe that's an awful lot of what they do in hospitals.'

'Castor oil,' said Donald reminiscently. 'I mind when I had my arm off the surgeon said I'd had too much castor oil. Likely I had, too, for I used to take a couple of big spoonful of it every few days then. I reckon that's what kept me fit while I was at the war, anyway.'

'A couple of spoonsful of it every few days!' remonstrated Anna Vic. 'Surely a body had no need of that amount at all?'

'Aye, well, the nurses tried to stop me but I didn't take any notice of them. Then when this surgeon was takin' the dressin' off my arm he said to me, "Donald," he says, "have you been taking castor oil?" "Aye," I told him, "I have a dose every now and then." "Good God, Donald!" he says. "You've been taking that much you've got it all through your system and it's comin' out of your arm here. You must stop it right away or it'll never heal." He showed me the dressin' with all this oil on it—you could see it plain as anythin'. That's as true as I'm here an' I've never taken another dose of castor oil since,' Donald concluded, taking a hearty bite out of a scone.

'Johnny wouldn't be needin' castor oil so long as he can get bakin'-soda,' said Morag, when we had digested Donald's story. 'The way that man eats it you'd surely wonder he had a stomach left.'

'It's a damty good stomach when you think what he puts into it,' Erchy defended as he got up to go and resume work.

Donald too stood up. 'I'd best go an' seek my arm,' he told us, 'for if I don't find it I'll need to get the doctor to give me a new one.'

'Best get him to give you a new head, then, while he's at it,' suggested Erchy impudently.

I was still thinking of Johnny Comic and of an article I had recently read which claimed that a Russian doctor had discovered that a daily dose of bicarbonate of soda prolonged life, and I mentioned this as we all straggled out into the garden, Morag and Anna Vic to take up the burden of their creels once more and Donald to continue his search for his hook.

'If that's true then Johnny Comic should live for another hundred years,' said Morag with a chuckle.

The next day Bruach was dumbfounded by the news that Johnny Comic had passed away during the night.

'An' did you hear what Kirsty said when she heard it?' Erchy demanded. 'She said, "Ach, he was always the same, any little thing killed him."'

We exchanged horrified glances.

'Aye, well,' resumed Erchy with complete matter-of-factness, 'I'm glad he's died in hospital so I won't have to go and shave him.'

'Why do you always go and shave people when they're dead?' I asked him curiously. 'Is it some superstition you have?' I was remembering that when Sandy had died Erchy had gone up to shave him on the day he died and then again on the eve of the funeral.

'But the beard grows after they're dead,' Erchy explained. 'An' these Seceders don't like the nurse to touch them once they've gone.'

I asked when the funeral was to be.

'It should be tomorrow,' he told me, 'but the undertaker sent word this mornin' that he was at a dance last night so he couldn't get the coffin ready in time. Now they're goin' to bury him on Thursday. We have to go tonight to dig a grave for him, though God knows where we'll find a place for him.'

'This village really does need a new burial ground,' I agreed. 'It's more like a rabbit warren than a cemetery.'

'Aye, an' the way you can hear the rabbits runnin' over the coffins in the graves there! It's terrible just.' He lit a cigarette. 'Aye, well, I expect we'll find a place for him up by the trees there. It's a bit away from the rest but I daresay there'll be others to keep him company soon enough.'

Thursday morning was full of early mist and when it had dispersed the heather clumps still held their nebulous quota in innumerable spiders' webs. Early mist usually presages a fine day and I hurried back from milking Bonny for, partly to see for myself Kirsty's reaction to the death of her brother and partly to please Morag, I had promised to go to the funeral. It was arranged that I should call for Morag at eleven o'clock but as I turned in at the gate of my cottage there was an agitated flutter of starlings from the rowan tree and I realized that, funeral or no funeral, unless

I gathered my rowanberries right away the birds would have stripped the lot before I returned. I put down the milk pail, grabbed a step-ladder and started to pick. There can be few sights more beautiful, more arresting, than a rowan tree in autumn with its profusion of red berries glowing against the tawny foliage. And Hebridean rowanberries seem to be so much more colourful than any others. As I harvested them I thought I had never seen them so vibrantly red as they were this year and looking at them in the palm of my hand I half expected to see their tiny pulses beating. When the basket was full there were still plenty left for the starlings and when, at the garden gate, I turned to look back at the cottage, the roof was spiky with birds awaiting my departure before re-commencing their banquet.

The first thing I noticed when Morag and I came in sight of Kirsty's cottage was the patch of bright colour where Johnny's garden had always been. I remarked on it to my companion.

'Aye, well, you mind Kirsty's cow has been that sick for two or three weeks past an' she's not had it stirrin' out of the byre.'

I didn't 'mind' for no one had thought to mention it.

'Poor Johnny,' I said. 'This must be about the first time he's managed to get flowers to bloom in his garden and now he's not here to see them.'

'Aye, it's a shame right enough,' agreed Morag. 'An' it's a shame about the beast too, for I'm hearin' she's not wantin' to eat anythin' let alone break into Johnny's garden to spoil his flowers for him.'

'They're lupins too,' I said as we drew near enough to identify them. 'I remember him telling me how the laird's gardener had given him some plants and he was so thrilled about it at the time.'

'An' just look at them,' Morag said. 'It's as though they know Johnny's dead for they're screamin' out loud with their bloomin'.'

The tiny kitchen of Kirsty's house was packed and overflowing with women all supporting or being supported by one another for everyone had been exceedingly fond of Johnny. The older women were dressed in black but the clothes of the younger women made a startling knot of colour in their midst. In front of the house the coffin lay across two kitchen chairs and the men stood in a semicircle round it, chattering among themselves and hunching their shoulders against a brisk breeze that burned their cigarettes away too quickly and scattered fragments of glowing red tobacco from their pipes. A couple of sheep dogs kept a wary eye on their masters and scratched themselves dispassionately. There was no sign of Kirsty.

A car drew up and the missionary got out and greeted the assembled crowd with what seemed to me to be unseemly levity. As he walked towards the coffin cigarettes and pipes were stubbed out. Swiftly there fell a silence that was broken only by the mournfully assertive song of a robin, the liquid call of an oystercatcher and the practised whimpering of a weep of Seceders who had detached themselves from the rest of the mourners.

'Where's Kirsty?' the missionary asked.

Everyone glanced about them as though they had not missed her until now and then someone spotted her coming away from the byre. She was dressed in black but her sleeves were rolled up and before she joined us she bent down and wiped her hands on the grass. We all guessed she had been ministering to her cow and there were whispers of enquiry to which she replied with a negative shake of her head. The missionary must have overheard them.

'Is your cow sick, then, Kirsty?' he demanded.

'Aye indeed,' replied Kirsty. 'I'm thinkin' she'll not last the day out.' Her voice was sufficiently funereal to convince everyone of her utter dismay.

'Oh, my, my,' said the missionary in shocked tones.

This particular missionary had often been described to me as 'a good missionary but a better cow doctor', so I was interested to see his reaction. He seemed to consider for a moment, and when he had made up his mind he snapped shut his book and laid it down on top of the coffin. 'Johnny has passed on,' he told us seriously, 'an' he'll take no harm from waitin' there while I go an' take a look at Kirsty's cow,' and rolling up the legs of his good black trousers he picked his way across the dungy path to the byre. Everyone followed in that direction.

'What ails the beast, d'you think, Kirsty?' he asked her.

'Indeed, but I don't know. She must have eaten somethin' strange, I'm thinkin'. She's been stuck fast for the last five days now an' nothin' the vet's sent will move her. I've been expectin' to find her gone each time I've come out to look at her.'

The byre was small and dark but we saw the missionary step over to the cow and feel her bones. Then he stepped back, pulled his black hat over his eyes a little and stared at the beast, biting his lips. Kirsty watched him intently and the mourners crowded closer to the door.

'Kirsty!' said the missionary at last, 'you're surely goin' to lose this beast.'

'Surely,' agreed Kirsty philosophically.

'Well then, as you're goin' to lose her in any case you'll no mind takin' a bitty risk with her?'

Kirsty nodded.

'Now, have you any Epsom salts?'

'Aye, I have some,' Kirsty told him.

'Well, you'll take two pounds of Epsom salts.' There was a gasp from the crowd. 'Now, repeat it as I say it so you'll not get it wrong,' the missionary instructed testily.

'I'll take two packets of Epsom salts,' faltered Kirsty, with unaccustomed submissiveness.

'Two pounds, woman!' the missionary shouted. 'Yon packets you get from the grocer is only about two ounces. You'll need sixteen of them. It's got to be kill or cure.'

'Two pounds of Epsom salts,' repeated Kirsty, meek as a child.

'And four pounds of margarine.'

'Four pounds of margarine.'

I felt Morag gripping my arm and there was no sound from the tense crowd round the door.

'Four pounds of treacle,' the missionary continued inexorably. 'An' when you've mixed them all together you can make it into balls and dip them into oatmeal and give them to her.'

'When will I give it to her?' Kirsty asked.

The missionary looked at the crowd and his eye lighted on Alistair. 'Alistair Mor Ruari!' he addressed him. 'You have long arms and no wife to be girnin' if you mess up your clothes so you can give her the dose right now while I'm here.'

The crowd relaxed and some of the women rushed off to collect the ingredients for the medicine. It seemed only a short time before they were back with a sticky-looking mess in a pail which Kirsty moulded into balls and handed to Alistair who rammed them down the cow's throat one by one.

'Now,' said the missionary when that was done. 'See that the last thing before you go to bed, Kirsty, if the beast's still alive, you'll give her a quart of linseed oil mixed with a pint of turpentine. Now promise you'll do that.'

'Tonight,' Kirsty said with steady emphasis, 'if the Lord spares me, I'll give her a quart of linseed oil and a pint of turpentine.'

'You mean if the Lord spares the cow,' murmured a familiar voice behind me. ''Tis no' you, Kirsty, who's takin' the dose.'

There was a faint titter from the crowd which was hushed immediately as the missionary rounded upon them.

'I'm thinkin',' he said, with gruesome practicality, 'if this beast dies in the night she'll be that swollen by mornin' you'll never get her out of this narrow doorway without cuttin' her to pieces first. You'd best just get her down to the bog where there's plenty of soft ground that'll make the buryin' of her easy.'

The men rallied round the cow and carried and pushed the poor emaciated creature down towards the bog. By the time they returned the missionary had reassumed an appropriately obsequial air and commenced to read the burial service.

'I was wonderin',' said Janet hesitantly to Morag and me as we watched the men carrying away the coffin for burial, 'Johnny bein' so fond of his flowers, would we pick them and put them on his grave?' As we approved her thought she suggested it to Kirsty who apparently agreed for a few moments later we saw them gathering armfuls of the blooms and then following the cortège down the road.

We walked home in the September sun, discussing the remarkable 'dose' the missionary had prescribed.

'I doubt the linseed oil alone will be enough to turn the beast inside out,' Morag predicted.

Early on Friday morning I began the rather tedious process of making rowan wine and was putting a great deal of energy into pulping the berries when Erchy arrived.

'Come an' we'll get your cupboard while the tide's high,' he said. 'It'll not be so far to carry it down the shore.'

On one of my beachcombing expeditions I had found washed up a very nice ship's locker which I thought would do very well for a cupboard in my kitchen. It was much too big and heavy for me to carry home alone so I had asked Erchy if he would come with me some time and we would get it home by boat.

We dragged the dinghy down the beach and while Erchy took the oars I huddled in the stern. The morning held the threat of rain over the grey water and the hills looked cold and snuffly with shreds of white cloud clinging about them like discarded paper handkerchiefs. Erchy was uncommunicative and the boat nosed forward with only the squeak of the oars in the rowlocks and the splash of the blades on the water for an accompaniment. A few lethargic raindrops fell, pitting the slack surface of the sea like the enlarged pores in an old woman's face.

Erchy's eyes suddenly became focussed on the land. 'That looks like Kirsty on the shore there,' he said. I twisted round on the thwart and espied a figure hurrying along the edge of the cliff and stopping every few minutes to peer down at the shore. 'I wonder what she's after,' Erchy mused.

'I think she's beckoning us to go in,' I said. 'Do you think she's all right?'

'We'd best go in and see, anyway,' Erchy replied. He steered the boat towards the shore and Kirsty scrambled agilely down the cliff and came towards us. Erchy got out and held the dinghy, greeting her with taut interrogation.

I was struck by her woebegone expression and the muted urgency of her voice. Only once before had I seen Kirsty looking so thoroughly discomfited and that had been when Erchy, stung by some innuendo she had made, had boldly taunted her in front of several people that he 'didn't believe she'd ever had a man up her skirts in her life'. Kirsty, utterly shamefaced, had admitted that she 'didn't believe she ever had'. Now it seemed, as she had not looked much affected by Johnny's funeral yesterday, that something equally disconcerting had happened.

'I've lost my cow,' she informed us in a stricken voice.

'Ach, well, you expected to. The missionary told you that yesterday,' retorted Erchy.

'I don't mean that. I'm sayin' I can't find her anywhere.'

Both Erchy and I stared at her with extravagant surprise.

'You cannot find her?' Erchy repeated.

'I've looked everywhere an' I cannot find the beast. Come an' see for yourselves.'

We pulled the dinghy above the tide and followed Kirsty to the bog where the cow had been left the previous evening.

There was no sign of the beast.

'My God! What's these?' ejaculated Erchy, bending down to peer at some hoofmarks scored deep into the bog. He scratched his head bewilderedly.

'It's as though somebody was after chasin' the beast,' suggested Kirsty.

'Indeed, if that dose has worked her I doubt she'll think she had the devil himself chasin' her,' he vouchsafed.

Together we followed the hoofmarks and they led us strangely enough towards the burial ground. I think even before we came in sight of it that Kirsty and I suspected what had happened.

'Somebody's left the gate open,' Kirsty said, and there was dread in her voice.

'Them damty flowers!' Erchy upbraided her. 'I said yesterday it was a daft idea an' I say it more so now.'

We stood in the open gateway of the burial ground and looked towards Johnny's grave, a little apart from all the other crowded graves. The cow stood beside it, sublimely chewing her cud. There was no sign of the lupins but all round and completely covering the grave there were seas and seas of manure, and the smell was appalling.

'Look at that, now,' said Erchy in an awestruck voice. 'You cannot say she's stuck now, anyway.'

'The defiler!' breathed Kirsty. 'What will folks say of me when they see I've let my cow defile my own brother's grave?' She became almost human in her anguish. 'What will the missionary say?'

'Ach, if you say nothin' the rain'll get rid of the manure for you, but you'd best get the beast out of the way pretty quick,' Erchy advised. Kirsty 'stood not upon the order of her going' and in a trice the cow was out of the burial ground and being driven up the road towards her byre.

Without a word Erchy closed the gate of the burial ground after us and we returned to the boat. When he had rowed a few strokes he rested on his oars. 'That's the queerest dose ever I heard of to cure a sick beast,' he said, his voice full of wonder. 'Man! But that must be a good cow doctor.' He resumed rowing again but his perplexed expression betrayed that he was still pondering the miracle of the cure.

By the time we reached home with the cupboard the rain was pouring unstintedly from a sagging grey sky. It continued over the weekend and on Monday morning Erchy, who had been doing some careful reconnoitring, reported that there was no longer any trace of manure to be seen at the burial ground. The village, if they noticed anything amiss, refrained from comment but the next time the missionary came out for a funeral he was heard impressing on Kirsty what a good man her brother must have been because the Lord had made the grass grow so much greener over and around his grave than anywhere else. He likened it to a 'green halo'.

Now in case any interested farmer should read this account perhaps I ought to mention that Kirsty's cow lived for seven years after this event had taken place and during that time she produced four good calves.

As though it may have some significance, Erchy insists that I also mention that the missionary died within two years!

X.   *All Mod. Cons.?*

THERE WAS NO SOUND OF RAIN on the roof when I woke but
the morning was damp and shot with chilliness, as though
winter were already licking its chops. Blessedly the wind
had dropped away to nothing so that, released from the
necessity of physical combat with it when I went outside, I
felt unburdened and relaxed. The cattle who had so long
confined themselves to grazing the sheltered corries in the
hills had moved upwards during the night so that they now
stood elegantly silhouetted along the skyline, a sight which
is locally believed to foretell a spell of fine weather. In a
sheltered corner of my garden a few bedraggled plants that
had waited so long for stillness opened their petals warily
in response to the tremors of sunlight that managed to evade
the glowering clouds.

I had planned a busy morning and was outside giving

the kitchen mats a thorough beating and shaking when I became aware of the sound of voices and, slipping with typical Bruach curiosity to the end of the house, saw Morag, Yawn and Erchy, each carrying a sack and a pail and looking very workmanlike in their whelking clothes, coming down the path.

'My, but you're starting the whelks early,' I called to them.

'Aye, indeed. But they're sayin' there's a good prices on them already,' returned Morag happily. 'You should be leavin' that an' comin' with us.'

I detest picking whelks. 'I'm going to do some washing while the rainwater tank is full,' I told them. 'I've left it far too long as it is.'

Morag accepted my excuse without comment. Yawn treated me to a sardonic stare.

'They're sayin' we're goin' to get the water at last,' rushed in Erchy consolingly, 'so you'll be able to wash whenever you feel like it then.'

'Are we really?' I demanded. 'Is it really true?'

'As true as I'm here,' declared Erchy with an air of misgiving. 'Did you no' have the wee mannie round askin' for your signature on a paper?'

I had indeed had the 'wee mannie' round but he had been almost gloatingly pessimistic as to the chance of the authorities piping water to my cottage in less than five years' time at least. The main obstacle, he had told me, was that the village was too scattered, thus making any scheme so far proposed too costly to be approved. Also, he had confided, not all the Bruachites considered piped water necessary, some of the more rigid Presbyterians maintaining that the Good Lord made the water to flow where He wanted it and therefore it was not right for Man to try to deflect its course, an attitude that I would have found too preposterous to believe had I not previously come up against it when the draining of a patch of boggy land had been proposed.

The 'mannie' had suggested that it might be worth my while to install a ram pump at the well down by the shore and pipe water to the cottage from it.

'I don't know if the supply would be adequate,' I had told him. 'It's a very shallow little well.' Very obligingly he had come with me to inspect it.

'I daresay the supply might be good enough if it was dug out a bit,' he suggested. 'But wait, now, till I test it.' Full of enthusiasm he had hurried back to his car, returning with a thin metal rod about four or five feet long with which he had proceeded to probe the depth of the well. It went down eventually to about two-thirds of its length.

'Just as I thought,' he told me cheerfully. 'You'd have plenty water there if you could get it dug out a bit more. It's just that it's all silted up with not being used for so long.'

I had been grateful for his encouragement and as we walked back to the car he had very kindly worked out for me the probable cost of the installation. 'Of course, you'll understand mine's only a very rough estimate,' he had cautioned. 'I don't really take anything to do with the water department at all. It's only that somebody's been badgering the Council about getting the water here and seeing I was coming out this way they asked me to collect signatures.'

'You're not from the water department then?' I had asked.

'No, no. Water's not my job at all.'

'Oh,' I said innocently, 'I assumed that you carried that rod with you for testing the depth of the wells so that you could advise people as to their suitability for providing a piped supply.'

'This rod? Oh, no indeed. This is a grave poker.' He wriggled it carefully into position across the seats of his car. 'You know,' he explained chattily, oblivious of the tenseness of the moment, 'there's a rule now that corpses must be buried four feet down. But they won't take any notice of it hereabouts if I don't go round all the burial grounds every so often and prod the graves to see how deep they've put them.'

'A grave poker?' I echoed.

'Yes, indeed.' He darted a suspicious glance at my face. 'I suppose it sounds kind of funny to you, being a stranger.'

I agreed that it did.

'Well, goodbye,' he said brightly, getting back into his car. 'I'm very pleased to have been able to help you.'

Back in the kitchen I had fortified myself with a cup of tea—made from rainwater.

'I don't believe they mean to give us the water at all,' said Morag, her voice full of scepticism. 'We've been promised it now for twenty-five years that I know of an' there's still no sign of it. I doubt I'll never see it in my time, anyway.'

'Damty sure you will,' replied Erchy with a surge of confidence.

Yawn still continued to stare at me with sardonic amusement but as the conversation seemed to have petered out and Morag and Erchy were starting to move away I began to shake some of the mud from my mats. Yawn still made no move to follow his companions, so I grinned at him fatuously, wishing he would say something or else go. A few more moments under his embarrassing scrutiny and I would be driven to asking him what was wrong. Suddenly he spoke.

'I'm thinkin' you must be one of them arishtocrats.'

It was my turn to stare. Anything less like an aristocrat than I looked at that moment in my gumboots, soiled overall, rubber gloves and with a muddy mat clutched in either hand I could not have imagined. 'Why do you say that?' I asked in undisguised bewilderment.

''Tis only arishtocrats that wears rubber gloves to shake mats,' he admonished me. 'Next thing we know you'll be takin' to cuttin' your peats with a knife and fork.' He permitted himself a short grunt of laughter. 'I knew some people once from hereabouts and they went to live for a time in Edinburgh. When they came back here they was that arishtocratic they put on gloves to eat their salt herrin'.' Satisfied now that he had made his criticism, but still mumbling condemnation, he turned to follow the other two.

I continued with my chores, speculating again as to the financial possibility of having my own piped water supply but it was indeed futile speculation for I had already come to the decision that it would cost more than I could afford.

I argued with myself that the energy used in carrying water could be so much more profitably spent in doing other things. I had learned to be frugal—water that had been used for my own toilet was then re-heated to wash towels, etc., and then tipped into a pail for washing floors. But it was not just the energy I grudged, it was the time it all took. I am not blessed with single-mindedness so that more often than not when I took up my pails and started to hurry to the well I would catch a glimpse of a strange bird, so that I had to freeze while I tried to identify it. Or, enchanted by the sight of greenfinches feeding on the seeds of the burdock plants that grew against the stone dykes, I would ignore the urgency of my task. Sometimes it was a new flower among the heather that caught my attention, or the particular shades and patterns of a mossy bank. Always there was so much wildness and beauty accompanying even the most mundane outside work and I could not bear to let myself pass it by.

Not for the first time I wished that the powers-that-be would get their priorities in order. It seemed to me ludicrous that electricity, which was well on its way to Bruach, should come before there was a prospect of a water supply, but that was what was happening in other less inaccessible villages so that it was not unusual to see bent old women tottering from a well, which was often no more than the most rudimentary depression in the ground, carrying the full pails of water back to their old-fashioned croft kitchens and there shakily ladling the water with the traditional tinker-made dipper into a shiny new electric kettle.

One or two families in Bruach already had a water supply, but they were the luckier ones who had wells close to their houses yet on higher ground so that it was an easy and relatively inexpensive matter to pipe the water. It is doubtful if even they would have bothered had they not intended to cater for summer tourists. The rest of the crofters, having carried water all their lives, suffered little frustration from the lack of it and though they would agree wholeheartedly, when the subject was mentioned at the ceilidhs, that it would 'indeed be wonderful to have the watter', their desire for it was never as fervent as my own. They professed to want bathrooms but more, I suspected, as a status symbol than a genuine need. Their attitude was in fact epitomized for me by old Murdoch who having heard he could get a grant to have a bathroom built on to his house applied for it immediately. Now Murdoch and his niece had been doing very well out of taking in boarders for bed and breakfast—'nighter's' they called them—and the wily Murdoch thought that if he could, without much cost to himself, get another room built on he could offer even more accommodation. He reckoned that once the bathroom was built he would only have to turn round to the authorities and tell them there was no water supply and they would just pay the grant and let him get away with it as an extra bedroom. It was unfortunate for Murdoch that a new inspector was appointed just about the time his so-called bathroom was completed and although it was furnished with a bowl on a stand, a pail of water and a towel rail Murdoch found it impossible to convince the inspector that the new building merited the description 'bathroom'. To the old man's dismay he was informed that the grant would be withheld until the room was equipped with a conventional bath, toilet basin and W.C. Vociferous with indignation Murdoch grudgingly complied and again approached the authorities, assuring them, no doubt in good faith, that he was willing to sign an undertaking that as soon as piped water was available in Bruach he would have it connected to his bathroom. He naturally did not disclose that in the meantime he intended to store the unusable mod. cons. in a shed and let the room as a bedroom to help pay for them. But the authorities were adamant. To qualify for the description 'bathroom' there must be running water. The inspector came to deliver the ultimatum to Murdoch when the old man was perched on a ladder repairing for the third time that season the damage the storms had done to his roof. Murdoch almost exploded. The inspector waited for him to subside and then pointed out helpfully that there was a good well not far away which could supply ample water without a great deal of expenditure. Murdoch, still spluttering with wrath and argument, descended the ladder and faced the inspector aggressively and then in truly Gaelic fashion, he flung out his arms in a dramatic gesture. 'Look at that!' he cried, pointing up at the roof. 'Look at it, will ye! Over fifty years me an' my father before me has been tryin' to keep the water from comin' into this house, an' now you're after forcin' me to take it in.' He had spat his disgust into the wind, chuckled appreciation of his own joke, and then invited the inspector inside for a strupak.

So Murdoch had 'taken in the watter' and no one was more proud than himself when it was finally installed. He had even announced his intention of taking a bath some day, the first in his long life. It was about six months afterwards that he had sprackled up to me when we were both out on the hill feeding our cattle in the misty quiet of the evening.

'Here, Miss Peckwitt,' his voice was hardly more than an awed whisper. 'Did you ever take a bath?'

'Yes,' I answered, knowing that if I betrayed the least surprise or amusement I should never know what lay behind the question.

'Well, tell me, when you came out of it did you no' feel like a herrin' that's been stripped of its scales just?' His blue eyes were anxious and expectant.

'I don't think so,' I said and this time I could not control a slight tremor in my voice.

'An' did you no' feel for a week or more after it as though your clothes was full of wee, wee splenters?' He wriggled with a suppleness that belied his age. I shook my head.

'Ach, well that's just the way I felt myself after it. Ach, I enjoyed it right enough when I was in it but I never want another one the way it left me feelin'.'

The day stayed calm and patchily bright. After lunch I got out 'Joanna', having promised to drive Katy, the shepherd's wife, and her half-sister, Ishbel, to a neighbouring village to visit a friend who had just moved into a newly built house. It had been arranged that I should pick them up at 'the back of three' and Ishbel was already waiting for me by the croft gate, dressed regally in her best clothes and carrying a string bag which contained a couple of small parcels. Whenever she visited a house, however briefly, Ishbel always took along some little gift. It was usually something quite trivial, perhaps a hank of darning wool, or a packet of envelopes, perhaps a magazine or even a packet of needles, just some little thing she found she could spare, so that she should never go empty-handed. Nervous, as always, she got into the car filling it with the evidence of her unstinted and relentless combat with the moths which she imagined campaigned against her with a vindictiveness that was purely personal.

At the shepherd's cottage we picked up the plump and voluble Katy who seemed to burst into chatter with every bump of the rough road. Ishbel said little and she was too shy even to respond to the convivial knots of workmen we passed, who took their weight off their spades to raise them in excited greeting—which, Katy observed derisively, was probably the most strenuous work they'd be doing that day. Despite the indolence of Highland labourers, however, progress was stalking rapidly towards Bruach, leaving a wake of tall poles which were to carry the electricity to the village. There were more signs of change too, for there was an extremely favourable grant and loan scheme for building new houses to replace the old croft dwellings, and the younger folk, though perhaps exiles themselves, had been quick to take advantage of it. The squat, tiny-windowed old croft houses, usually built in the most sheltered corner of the croft, were becoming byres for cattle while beside them desirable two-storey residences with modern steel windows were appearing, looking as exposed and uncomfortable as someone who has just been kicked out of a warm bed. Into these the old people moved reluctantly, complaining of their coldness and temporarily overawed by their comparative spaciousness and by the sight of the bathrooms and up-to-the-minute sink units complete with mixer taps—though of course they still had neither water nor drainage.

It was beside such a cluster of raw-looking houses that I brought 'Joanna' to a stop and Maggie, a dumpy, merry-voiced little woman with almost no inhibitions, rushed out to greet us effusively. Ishbel presented her gifts—a packet of biscuits and a tin of condensed milk—both of which were opened immediately and offered to us. We sat in the white glossy kitchen and drank tea while Maggie entertained us with a fluent and descriptive recital of all the events that had taken place in the village of recent months. She told us, with many interpolations from Katy, of Padruig Mor, who had been to the mainland to attend an auction sale where he had bought himself an old grandfather clock.

'Ach, it was no bloody good at all,' said Maggie. (It is not usual to hear a Hebridean woman swear but the fact that Maggie did so unrestrainedly seemed, so far as her neighbours were concerned, to enhance her attraction as a hostess.) 'Indeed,' she continued, 'the works was all gone out of it long since but he brought it home with him on the train as proud as a cockerel.' I recollected Padruig Mor's tiny, dark old house, commonly described as a 'wee but and ben', and so was not surprised when Ishbel asked: 'How in the world did he get it into his house?'

'He didn't to begin with,' replied Maggie, shrill with ridicule. 'The ceilin' was too low, so what did my fine fellow do but dig a hole in the floor till the clock would fit it. It's daft he is surely.'

'So grandfather has one foot in the grave already,' I murmured.

'So he has. You should go and see it for yourselves. It looks crazy just but he's that pleased with it,' said Maggie. 'Aye, but it was a laugh, I can tell you.'

Ishbel, Katy and she fell to discussing the rest of the neighbours, politely drawing me into the conversation when it seemed I had been silent too long, although most of the names they referred to I had heard of only vaguely, if at all. Despite the fact that I had not taken off my coat I felt cold, for the room was too large to be heated adequately by the discreet little grate that peeped out of the ultra-modern tiled surround, although Maggie had it piled high with peats. The room was full of such contradictions. The fireplace was flanked by battered pails of peats and the miniature mantelpiece was decorated with imposing silver ornaments that looked as though they might have been filched from a hearse. On the spotless hearth two black iron pans stood and a bundle of hen feathers lay ready for sweeping up any fallen ash. The centre of the room was taken up by a plastic-topped table with metal legs but the solid old croft-house bench was backed along one wall, throne-like in its austerity. Above it a bundle of rabbit skins hung from the ceiling. Everywhere looked scrubbed and clean, the new linoleum on the floor being still smeared with damp from a recent washing and even as I watched a grey-looking cat sidled apprehensively from under the bench and then streaked out through the open door as if it too expected to be picked up and scrubbed.

Maggie filled an old black kettle from one of the enamel pails which stood in the stainless steel sink and poised it delicately half on, half off the fire with the remark that she didn't see the use of these sort of fireplaces anyway, what was the use of a fire that didn't boil the bloody kettle?

'Don't you use the electric kettle?' Katy asked.

'I can never find a match to light it with,' retorted Maggie, and when we had finished laughing, she went on: 'The bugger won't let me use it. He says I'll likely burn the bottom out of it.' The outrage in her voice was only for our benefit.

'The bugger', her son Seoras, appeared in the doorway at that moment. He was a dark, wiry young man with a permanently satirical expression on his face and a tongue even less inhibited than his mother's. However, he greeted us with perfunctory politeness as he threw off his jacket and sat down at the table. Maggie scooped a steaming bowl of unpeeled potatoes from one of the pots on the hearth and ladled a mound of boiled fish on to a plate from the other one and placed them in front of Seoras. He bent to his repast with great concentration.

'Will you come and see over the house?' invited Maggie, and led us first to the blue and white tiled bathroom which contained, besides an aridly futile-looking W. C., a bath so narrow that anything but the slimmest of figures would have needed the aid of tyre levers to get in or out.

'That's a useful cupboard you have there, under the washbasin,' I observed. 'Much better than being able to see all the pipes.'

'Indeed it is,' agreed Maggie, and opened the door to reveal a broody hen sitting tight on a clutch of eggs. 'It's a grand little cupboard,' she enthused.

We followed her into a downstairs bedroom and then into another room, not yet furnished.

'Which room is this to be?' I asked.

Maggie hesitated a moment or two before replying.

'Indeed, I don't know just what he called it,' she admitted. 'Seoras!' she screamed back into the kitchen. 'What did they call this room on the plan?'

'Damned if I know,' responded Seoras thickly.

'Wait now till I get the plan and then you'll tell me,' said Maggie, rushing off. She returned and handed me a rolled-up plan which we studied for a moment together.

'This will be the sitting-room, then,' I hazarded.

'The sitting-room?' she repeated guilelessly. 'Is that what they call it? Indeed, God knows what we'll put to sit in here unless it's more dockin' hens.'

'D'you hear that, Seoras—it's the sitting-room,' she called.

'No, it is not, then—the shitting-room is the one with the bath in it,' retorted Seoras.

Upstairs there were three bedrooms, more than Maggie

had known in her life although she had brought up seven children. 'It's kind of lonely, though,' she said regretfully when we exclaimed over their proportions. All the windows were curtained with net, shutting out the glorious view and to me it seemed a pity that the crofter wife should emulate the townswoman in that the bigger windows she aspires to the more curtaining she buys to screen them. I drew aside one of the bedroom curtains to look out across the shaggy moors, smouldering with autumn colour, to where the mist-wreathed hills looked down sulkily at the restless water. My three companions came up behind me.

'I see old Flora and Jamesie didn't take to livin' in their new house yet,' observed Katy, pointing to a brash new dwelling beside an old croft house on which a sagging roof seemed to have settled with much the same brooding determination as the hen I had just seen on the clutch of eggs in the bathroom.

'No, and I don't believe they ever will,' Maggie asserted.

'I wonder why?' I mused.

'Ach, I think they're afraid of dirtying it,' was Maggie's pert rejoinder.

It was time for us to go, and we returned to the kitchen to collect Ishbel's bag and my gloves.

'I must pee before I go,' announced Ishbel with perfect naturalness.

'Of course,' said Maggie hospitably, and led us out to the back of the house where a new concrete cattle byre of approved hygienic design had replaced the former dry-stone byre. Straddling the dung trench behind the incurious cows we relieved ourselves.

'It's handy, this,' Katy approved.

'Ach, aye, it's better by far than the old place,' replied Maggie seriously.

Seoras was standing beside the rainwater tank, scrubbing at his face with a tatter of towel.

'If you're goin' back to Bruach now, I was just thinkin' I might get a lift with you,' he said. 'It's time I got myself a haircut.'

'Seoras!' expostulated his mother, 'you can't go yet, you didn't milk the cow.'

'Milk her yourself, you lazy old cailleach,' replied Seoras with complete bonhomie. He picked up a bottle of beer from the kitchen table and followed us outside.

'Seoras!' his mother screamed after him. 'You didn't get the peats.'

Seoras responded with a spate of Gaelic too fluent for me to understand.

'Seoras, you're a b—' Maggie clapped her hand over her mouth and looked contrite. 'Oh, Seoras boy, I nearly called you a bad name.'

'Aye, I know,' Seoras returned with a bleak smile. 'You nearly called me a bugger.'

'Oh, no, Seoras,' she rectified, 'I nearly called you a bastard.'

They were still hurling insults at each other with perfect good humour when we drove away with Seoras in the back seat beside Ishbel.

'Isn't it a good thing there's a right barber now in Bruach

after all these years,' offered Ishbel timidly, for the presence of a male always overawed her. 'Is he a good barber would you say?'

'I don't know,' interposed Katy, 'but,' she added as if in commendation, 'they all say he's a good sheep shearer, anyway.'

It was only during the last year that Bruach had acquired a barber when a crofter exile who claimed to have had barbering experience in Glasgow came home to spend his retirement on his sister's croft. Some said he had never been more than temporary lather boy and that fifty years ago, but whatever qualifications he may or may not have possessed he had announced his willingness to give any man a haircut or a shave. So as to run no risk of his earnings interfering with his pension he would accept only a pint of beer in recompense for his services. To the gratification of his lonely widowed sister and the corresponding envy of neighbours the barber's house had soon become a popular ceilidh house where there was always a good gathering of men not only from Bruach but from other barberless villages desiring to have their hair cut. His shaving was not nearly as much in demand, and those who had undergone the experience did not choose to repeat it, complaining that the barber 'kept a bloody cuckoo in a clock that burst out every quarter of an hour and made you jump so much you were feart where the razor would land next.'

As we were depositing Ishbel outside her home a sauntering figure approached us. It was Erchy, just returning from his whelking. Seoras poked his head out of the car to talk to him.

'Are you here just to ceilidh then, or are you goin' some place?' Erchy asked him.

'I'm here to see will the barber cut my hair for me,' replied Seoras.

Erchy lifted his cap and felt his own mop of hair experimentally. 'I could do with a haircut myself,' he admitted, 'an Johnny's supposed to be bringin' me out some of that stuff on the bus tonight.' He nodded towards the bottle of beer in Seoras's lap.

'A bottle of beer is very cheap for a haircut, isn't it?' I asked.

'I got a haircut and three dirty stories for my pint last time,' said Seoras. 'That's good value if you like.'

'Aye,' admitted Erchy cautiously, 'it's good value right enough but all the same, sometimes if there's been a few there before you so you're at the end of the queue, it's a damty queer haircut you get out of it.'

XI. *Love and Coal*

'THERE,' SAID YAWN, with a satisfied grunt. 'You'll not take those out with your teeths.'

I concealed a smile. 'No,' I agreed, though I doubted if his handiwork was really any more robust than my own. Yawn had found me trying to repair the drooping boards of my peat shed when he had come to deliver a piece of his sister Sarah's home-made haggis. With uncharacteristic gallantry he had seized the hammer when I laid it down for an instant and, without comment, had continued to hammer in the nails himself.

'That should stand for a while,' I acknowledged by way of gratitude, having learned that to offer Yawn direct thanks only embarrassed and confused him.

He walked around the shed, aiming experimental kicks at the walls. 'You'll be needin' a new shed anyway before long,' he warned me. 'You cannot expect this one to stand up to much in the way of weather.'

I shrugged my shoulders. 'It'll have to stay until it blows away or falls down,' I told him. 'I can't afford to build a new one.'

'If you could put some stones round it just, to strengthen it,' he suggested. 'It might do you a wee bitty longer.'

'And where do I get the stones?' I asked him resignedly.

Yawn plunged his hands into his pockets with an air of finality. 'Aye,' he conceded, 'that's the way of it just.'

Despite the rocky ground, the craggy cliffs and the boulder-strewn shores, suitable stones for building were scarce enough in Bruach. There was an abundance of round stones, or oval stones, or sausage shaped stones, all moulded to smooth symmetry by the sea or by the rushing burns, but flat stones such as could be built into a wall were precious and if you had any on your croft you hoarded them jealously for the day when you would surely need them. They might be required in times of storm for weighting down haystacks or perhaps the roof of your house (it is difficult for an amateur to tie a rope successfully to a round stone). One of pleasing shape and size might even be used as a headstone for a grave for few Bruachites wasted money on expensive tombstones. And of course the local lobster-fishermen were constantly on the look-out for good stones for their creels. Indeed so rapacious were they that it had been reported from some villages that the fishermen were suspected of helping themselves to headstones from the burial grounds. Erchy maintained the report was more than suspicion and claimed to have seen a creel newly hauled from the sea in which a couple of good-sized lobsters were crawling over a stone roughly carved with the words 'Isobel C . . . aged 89 yrs'. Erchy said he couldn't have eaten those lobsters 'supposin' you'd given him a bottle of the "hard stuff" [whisky overproof] to wash the taste out of his mouth afterwards'. And yet though stone in Bruach was so scarce there was on nearly every croft at least one tumbled ruin of a dry-stone house or shed which, curiously enough, no one ever tampered with. There was just such a ruin in a corner of my own croft, now smugly canopied with many decades of moss and fern growth, but when I had one day embarked on the task of levering up some of the stones from their settled positions with the avowed intention of strengthening my peat shed in just the way Yawn was now suggesting, he himself had soon appeared on the scene to exhort me not, on any account, to disturb the stones.

'But they're not doing any good there, are they, Yawn?' I had argued, suspecting that it was either sheer sentiment or the possible disturbance of the 'wee folk' that prompted his concern.

'Aye, but you'd best not lift them,' he had insisted. 'You'll lift those stones and you'll lift a fever.'

'A fever?' I echoed. 'Why?'

'Ach, well, that was one of the houses that was left at the time of the big fever when it was in these parts,' he had explained. 'They set fire to all those that had it but the fever still stays in the stones so they say.' His voice was exceedingly grave. 'Nobody about here believes in touchin' them, anyway.'

'Do you remember this big fever, Yawn?' I had asked him.

'No, but I mind my father tellin' me of it. He remembered it from when he was a lad just.'

As soon as Yawn had gone I had dismissed his warning as absurd and had carried the few stones I had already prised out over to the peat shed. They were extremely heavy and the muscles of my back began to object so strongly that I had given up work for the rest of the day. That night I had been unable to sleep because of the agonizing pain in my back and next morning I had felt as though I was developing all the symptoms of a severe cold. However, within a day or so I was perfectly all right again and I returned to the task of further depleting the ruin. I had succeeded in dislodging several more stones before my back had again begun to trouble me and a sneaky chillness had insinuated itself between my shoulder blades. I had left off work and gone back to the cottage to get warm but though there were no other recognizable symptoms of a cold the chillness refused to be thawed by hot drinks sipped before a roasting fire with my back as the main target for the heat, and it remained icily indifferent to a 'poultice' of a hot-water bottle tucked under my bedjacket; for three days I was subject to sudden fits of shivering. As soon as I had recovered I resolved that when a reasonable day came I would continue work on the ruin, and told myself with great firmness that my aches and pains were either the direct result of perspiring freely while working in heavy clothes and then standing about in a bleak wind, or else they were of psychological origin. For how, I asked myself, could fever linger in stones to remain a source of infection a century or so later? There had come a day of relative mildness with a ragged sky that looked like old sheep's fleece and a spectral breeze that breathed moistly on the rusty sedge. I approached the ruin with waning confidence, for it seemed to my doubtless prejudiced eye to have taken on a slightly sinister aspect, the dark cavities from which I had already removed the stones looking like resentful scars on the ageing skin of moss. It is easy enough to shrug off apprehension or superstition in the warm comfort of one's own kitchen when one has just switched off 'Woman's Hour'; not so easy when one is completely alone with the wildness of the moors where even the straightening of the trodden grass dogs one's footsteps with stealthy whispers. Strangely loath to start work I prospected for a place where the dislodging of one stone might release several more and thus quicken my labours but they seemed to be embedded more firmly than I remembered and when I thought I had found such a place I had not the strength to move a single stone. My back began to ache in anticipation and I could have sworn I felt the first vestige of a shiver. I had looked sourly at the ruin and then sorrowfully towards my flimsy peat shed. Then I had gone back to the cottage and started to bake bread.

'Aye,' repeated Yawn, pushing vigorously at the peat shed again. 'There's not many stones hereabouts that you can use.' We had carefully turned our backs on the ruin, which I never interfered with again. 'You could get a few from the shore maybe if you looked long enough,' he added.

'It isn't often one sees a flat stone on the shore,' I objected.

'Ach, you'd find flat ones if you looked for them. Other folks does. Look at Alasdair there,' he went on. 'Every day he goes to the shore and finds himself a good stone or two to carry up in his creel for this wall he's after buildin'.' There was a glint of amusement in Yawn's eye.

'That's so,' I admitted. Every day, whatever the weather, one could see the indomitable Alasdair struggling up the cliff path from the shore with one or two stones each weighing nearly half a hundredweight in a creel on his back. These he would painstakingly build into the very substantial wall that had been destined originally to protect the tiny flower garden his Glasgow-born wife had once dreamed of planting. Perhaps, when he had dedicated himself to it over fifty years ago as a young man of twenty-four, the task had not seemed to him so stupendous but even now though he rarely missed a day during all that time the wall still needed many stones to complete it. But, though his wife had been dead for some years, he still plodded doggedly on. Perhaps he was impelled by the desire to fulfil a promise made to his deceased wife; perhaps it was too difficult to break the self-imposed routine of a lifetime, but whatever the reason Alasdair's wall still continued to grow by that daily quota of hard-won stones.

'It passes the time for him,' Yawn said with true Gaelic understanding of his need. I suspected that if the wall were ever completed Alasdair might find there was no purpose left in living.

Being blessed with neither Alasdair's rugged physique nor the Bruachites' subjugation of time I knew that any flat stones I might find on the shore would stay there long enough to be washed into round ones before I would exert myself to carry them. My peat shed would have to take its chance in the gales.

'Well, are you thinkin' of buildin' Miss Peckwitt a new shed?' Morag came upon us in the midst of our ponderings and Yawn, no doubt fearing that I might take her remark seriously, hastily left us.

'I've brought you a wee bitty meat will do for your dinner.' Morag handed me a basin with half a dozen fresh chops in it.

'It's wonderful to have fresh meat,' I said gratefully, thinking how lucky I was to have a respite from the limp and unidentifiable chunks of flesh with gory paper clinging tenaciously that came to us through the post each week from the mainland butcher.

'Aye, mo ghaoil,' she rejoined devoutly, 'an' once you've eaten heather-fed lamb you're spoiled for any other meat for the rest of your life.'

Together we walked back to the cottage. 'I'll take the bowl back with me just,' said Morag. 'I'm thinkin' I'll take a wee taste over to Willy's wife, the poor soul.'

'How is Willy?' I asked as I rinsed out the basin. 'The poor man seems to be lingering on a long time, doesn't he?'

'Aye,' she agreed, with an anxious frown. 'He doesn't just seem as though he can make up his mind to die.' We heard the latch of the gate click and both turned to look out of the window. 'Here's Erchy,' she announced unnecessarily, 'an' I daresay he's come to bring you a piece of meat from his own beast. He was after killin' it a day or two since.'

'My goodness!' I said, 'I shall be able to feast for a week.'

As soon as the weather was cold enough for the flies to have disappeared and for meat to be kept safely for two, perhaps three, weeks in an ordinary shed, each Bruach family liked to slaughter a sheep. It was the custom then to give joints to one's friends who had not yet slaughtered and they would reciprocate when their turn came to kill. In this way the supply of fresh meat was prolonged for several weeks. I had no sheep but that did not deter my friends from bestowing upon me more than adequate joints as well as generous slices of haggis or blackpudding as they made them, for when a sheep was slaughtered the thrifty Bruach housewives saw that the entrails were eaten before the carcase was cut into at all. Yawn's sister, Sarah, easily the thriftiest woman in Bruach, had once told me that she used every bit of a sheep except for the ears and teeth and when I had asked for a demonstration she had taken me, in company with two pailsful of internal organs, down to the burn which bounded her croft. There, standing in icy cold water with the noisome contents of several stomachs and many yards of intestine swirling greenly around our gumboots, I was initiated into the mysteries of making haggis and blackpudding.

'There,' approved Sarah, when we were back in her

kitchen and the lungs of the sheep were simmering in a saucepan and dribbling pink froth from the trachea which was draped over the side of the pan, 'you'll be able to call yourself a right crofter now that you've helped clean a sheep and make a haggis.' I managed a wan smile but not until the blood had been mixed with oatmeal and poured into one stomach bag to be boiled into blackpudding, and the lungs and a selection of other dubious-looking morsels had been chopped up and stuffed into another stomach bag to be boiled into a haggis had I felt sure enough of my legs to rise from my chair and go to the door, desperate to breathe unfouled air again. But Sarah had been determined that I should witness every aspect of her skill and economy and the two collaterals were rubbing tumid shoulders in an enormous cauldron under the scrutiny of a singed sheep's head awaiting its turn beside the fire before she had allowed that the demonstration was over.

The following day when the haggis was cooled and set Sarah had sent me a thick slice of it which I crisped in the frying pan and then ate with some mashed potatoes. To my great surprise I had enjoyed every scrap of it and from that day on have been a devotee of the beast.

Erchy came into the kitchen and deposited a now familiar-looking parcel on the table. 'There's your ration,' he said to me and then, so as to foil any attempt at thanking him, he went on quickly: 'I'm just hearin' that Murdoch's been taken awful bad and they've had to send for the nurse.'

'Oh, be quiet!' ejaculated Morag with startled incredulity.

'Aye, it's right enough,' affirmed Erchy.

'Indeed, he was tellin' me only yesterday he'd been con-scripted for the best part of a week and the nurse had given him five calomel to shift him,' Morag remembered. 'Would it be to do with that likely?'

Erchy shook his head. 'I don't know at all,' he said. 'But what I'm after wonderin' now is whether the third one's not goin' to be Willy as we've all been expectin'.'

'Here, here,' murmured Morag in a horrified voice.

Erchy was of course referring to the old belief that graves were always required in threes. 'Once you've opened up the burial ground you'll need to open it up twice more,' he had told me. Although it was uncanny how often it came true it was a cruel superstition for once the first of the cycle of deaths had occurred the old folks in the village would begin to show distinct signs of uneasiness, even panic, un-til the third grave was satisfactorily filled when those that were 'spared' would shed their fears and with them many of their years and begin what was literally a new lease of life.

During the previous few weeks the Bruach burial ground had been opened twice—once for a young baby who had 'died of an open window' and once for Johnny Comic. Willy, who everyone knew could not last much longer, had been confidently accepted as the likely occupant for the third grave but in view of Erchy's news it was possible that Murdoch might be the third corpse and when Willy died he would likely be the first of another trio. Both Erchy and Morag looked very serious indeed. I tried to take their minds off the subject.

'I wish there was something I could do for you in return for all this lovely meat,' I said, with genuine wistfulness.

'Ach, 'tis nothin' at all,' Morag dismissed the suggestion instantly.

'Well, you can do somethin' for me,' said Erchy with a boldness he sometimes assumed in company. 'You can bake me a loaf of that nice bread you make. I reckon it agrees with my stomach better than shop bread.'

I had never known Erchy to refuse at least one slice of my homemade bread even if he had just taken his dinner when it was offered to him. 'I'll certainly do that,' I told him. 'But I'll let you into a secret, Erchy.' He looked at me curiously. 'The reason for the nice flavour of my bread is that I mix a handful of the hens' bran into the flour when I make it.'

'Is that right?' queried Morag.

'That's right,' I told her.

'I'd still eat it supposin' it was a handful of the hens' dung you mixed in with it,' said Erchy staunchly. 'It's damty good bread anyway.'

'Talkin' of bakin',' said Morag with careful offhandness. 'Were you no speakin' of givin' a party a while back.' She enunciated the word 'party' with the awkward amusement she assumed when she used a word she regarded as being 'swanky'.

'Yes, I was,' I replied. 'I've been wondering about the best time to have it.'

'Wait you, now,' said Erchy. 'If you go an' get all ready

to have a party an' then Willy goes an' dies, there's nobody would be able to come to it.'

I had already thought of that, Willy being related to every family in the village so that no household would be unaffected by his death.

'Ach, but that would be awful spiteful of the man to go an' die on you like that,' said Morag with just a trace of outrage in her voice.

'Aye, but he might do it, just the same,' Erchy warned her.

'Aye, so he might,' agreed Morag.

'Perhaps I'd better put it off altogether,' I suggested.

'Here, no!' said Erchy. 'There's no need to do that. Will your cakes no' keep for a wee whiley after you've baked them?'

'Yes, of course,' I told him; 'they'd keep for a few days anyway.'

'Well then,' said Erchy, 'you go ahead an' have your party and supposin' Willy dies we'll have him buried in a day or two an' then we could all come.'

Thus encouraged I went ahead and arranged to have what I had to refer to as a 'good ceilidh' on the Thursday of the following week. I started the necessary baking on the Tuesday so that there would be plenty of time for icing and decorating the various cakes. On the Wednesday morning Erchy called in to tell me that Willy had 'passed on' in the night. The funeral was to be on Friday.

'You'd best put off your party till Friday night now,' he advised me.

'But will people come to a party the same day as the funeral?' I asked him, more to reassure myself than from actual doubt in the matter.

Erchy's eyes opened wide in surprise. 'Surely they will,' he replied without a trace of hesitation. 'What would be keepin' them back then?'

I was about to comment on Willy being the occupant for the third grave when Erchy observed with great satisfaction: 'Well, we've got our third corpse all right. I'm tellin' you it always goes in threes.'

'You'll have another grave to dig tonight, then, will you?' I asked him.

'No,' he answered surprisingly. 'He's not to be buried here at all. Seemingly he left a wish to be put over in a burial ground on the mainland where his mother and his brother is buried already.'

'Does that mean you'll still be expecting to have a third grave to dig soon? You've always said it was the burial ground that had to be opened three times.'

'Aye, well,' he excused himself. 'When anybody dies I just straightway think of diggin'. It's just my own way of speakin' of it.'

My mind flashed to the other invalid. 'By the way, how's old Murdoch?' I enquired.

'Ach, there's nothin' wrong with him at all. Nothin' that a day out in the heather didn't cure anyway. He was there squattin' that long he took his oilskin with him an' made a tent of it. By God! but those calomel went through him. He was feelin' pretty bad when he got back an' didn't move from the fire until he heard this mornin' that Willy was dead. As soon as he heard that he was away out to see to his horse. His niece said she couldn't keep him back at all.' Erchy chuckled. 'I saw him myself out there, so I called out to him, "Murdoch, what are you at? I thought you was dyin'." He turned on me an' he shouted: "I'm no' dyin' yet. I'm owed too much money to die yet." "Who's owin' you money?" says I. "The government," he says. "Haven't I been payin' into that pension scheme for most of my life an' I'm damty sure I'm not goin' to die till I've had every penny of it back again."' Erchy shook his head. 'He's a hardy all right,' he said admiringly.

I left Erchy to spread the message that the ceilidh was to be postponed until the Friday evening and though I carried on with the preparations I could not help wondering if he had really spoken for the rest of the crofters and if I and the hens were to be left to eat our way through batch after batch of cakes and scones and tarts. Experience had shown me that there was always a terrific sense of relief in the village after a corpse was buried and that the subsequent ceilidhs were perceptibly more animated than usual but whether an arranged party would be considered too frivolous to follow directly upon a funeral I had yet to discover.

At about twelve o'clock on the Friday morning, whilst I was replenishing Bonny's manger with summer-smelling hay pulled from the middle of the stack I noticed an unfamiliar vehicle on the road and guessed that it was something to do with the funeral. A little later a few solemnly garbed people trickled homewards across the crofts and there was a busy hurrying of smoke from chimneys as everyone put their potatoes on to cook. The afternoon settled itself tranquilly over Bruach, the breeze of the morning having died away so that the cottage chimneys smoked in sleek blue plumes and the stilled moors relaxed for an hour in the discreet wintry sunshine. Only the figures of the women were to be seen going about their chores until just before dusk the small troupe of children straggled up the brae from school, their clamorous voices striking shrill echoes from the rough stone walls of the dykes.

At nine o'clock in the evening with the furniture pushed to one side and the refreshments laid out I was waiting a little tensely for the arrival of the first of my guests. The fire was sluggish for despite frenzied appeals to the new coal merchant I had received no delivery of coal for nearly six months and was having to make do with dross fortified by that summer's damp peats. It is a great disadvantage to have a coal merchant who is also a fish-salesman and a caterer for tourists, for when there is an abundance of either he cannot be persuaded to bother himself with the far less profitable coal. Fretfully I picked up the bellows which, like my copper warming pan, I had once bought as an antique but now found I needed to use frequently. I blew steadily on the fire and was soon rewarded by the sight of little spurts of flame that irradiated the shaggy peats into racing patterns of sparks. I was still blowing when my ears caught the noise of an engine in the distance and, throwing on a coat, I went outside to look. A pair of headlights was glaring down the road towards the cottage and a few minutes later a heavy lorry swung through the entrance to my croft. The driver, a blond young man with an impudent smile, jumped down.

'I've brought you the half-ton of coal you were wanting,' he told me in a voice that was as spiky as if he habitually dined on cactus.

'Oh, bless you!' I exclaimed with a delight that was not wholly due to the fact that I now had some coal. Since coming to live in Bruach where one had to fetch and carry so much for oneself the delivery of even the most utilitarian commodities filled one with excitement.

'Will you give me a light?' he asked and when, with slightly less excitement, I agreed, he pressed a torch into my hand and hauled himself up into the back of the lorry. There he commenced shovelling out the coal into a heap on the frosty grass. It was bitterly cold to be standing about and it seemed to take hours before the last shovelful of coal had clattered on to the heap and the shovel had been thrown back into the lorry.

'I must fill a pail and put some on the fire,' I said, shivering. 'You'd better come in and have a strupak.'

Chivalrously he offered to fill the pail for me and just as I was handing it out to him we discerned several torch flashes. From somewhere along the road came bursts of shouting and laughter. 'There's people comin' here,' the driver informed me needlessly.

'Yes,' I told him. 'They're coming to ceilidh with me. Stay if you'd like to.' I set the already singing kettles back on the stove and within a few moments heard the approaching thud of boots on the frosty ground followed by a heavy thump on the door. 'Come in!' I called, and they all pushed one after another into the tiny porch, their faces frost-whipped into enviable ruddiness. Whispering and commenting excitedly, those who wore coats took them off, dropped them on the stairs and then spread themselves over the room until all the available seats were taken and some of the girls were perched awkwardly two on a chair. The lorry driver dumped the pail of coals beside the fire and then sat himself on the floor beside the pouffé on which the attractive Mora was sitting. I met smiles with smiles and tried to make everyone as comfortable as space would allow but I was rather disappointed to note that except for the lorry driver and the old men—Yawn, Ian and an exceedingly sprightly Murdoch—the rest of my guests were female. The best ceilidhs were always those where the numbers were more or less equal and I hoped it would not be long before the rest of the men arrived.

'Where are Erchy and Hector and the rest?' I asked Morag as we handed round refreshments.

'Indeed I don't know at all,' she replied, genuine mystification in her voice. 'I don't believe they got back from the funeral yet.'

'Trust Erchy,' I said with some asperity. 'It was he who insisted on my going ahead with this party.'

'Here, mo ghaoil, but there's plenty of time for them yet,' she soothed.

After an hour or so had gone by and there was still no sign of the younger men the girls, except for Mora who was flirting modestly with the lorry driver, were beginning to look anxious, and though there was plenty of chatter and laughter it was possible in odd moments to hear the hiss of the pressure lamp which, to me anyway, meant that the party was not as successful as I had hoped it would be. However, Morag coaxed Murdoch into giving us a song and soon we were all joining in the choruses rapturously, the girls throwing back their heads and swaying and the old people beating their hands into their laps in time to the music. It was nearing midnight and we were in the middle of a particularly nostalgic Gaelic air when the door was flung open and Erchy and Hector and a bevy of the young men of the village tumbled in, their eyes shining, their caps pushed back on their heads and the pockets of their best suits bulging with bottles of various sizes.

'I thought you'd been to a funeral,' I commented as they sat themselves on the floor, their backs against the wall, and tucked hungrily into the food that was offered them.

'So we have,' responded Erchy happily. 'An' a right time of it we had too.' He looked at Hector and they grinned at each other with amiable understanding. 'We got that much of a surprise when we saw it was a bus that came to take the coffin to the funeral,' Erchy confided in a voice that effectively silenced everyone else in the kitchen. 'We was thinkin' it would be only a small car just to take the coffin and maybe one or two folks along with it. When we saw it was a bus an we could all go, we rushed away home to get a pound or two to put in our pockets. Seein' we was all dressed up anyway we thought we might as well go an' have a good drink.' He filled his mouth with a sandwich and spoke thickly through it. 'I'm tellin' you, Miss Peckwitt, if it hadn't been that I remembered about your party there's not one of us would have been back yet.'

'How did you get back?' I asked.

'We hired a car from that Farquhar man,' Erchy told me. 'I believe we started off fairly early but Farquhar would have us keep stoppin' for a drink. Honest,' he said in awe-struck tones, 'I've never known a car that does more pubs to the mile than that one of his.'

'Aye,' chimed in Hector, 'and tse more Farquhar's had to drink tse slower he drives. Indeed I was tsinkin' we'd get back sooner if we pushed. You'd tsink it was goin' to a funeral we was instead of comin' back from one, tse way he was drivin'.' He held his cup of tea at arms length and looked at it with much the same expression of distaste as I have seen on the face of a publican when he looks at a glass of his own beer.

With the arrival of the more virile men the girls shed the last remnants of lassitude and the inevitable teasing and chaffing began. Bottles were flourished, glasses were demanded; the singing became progressively louder and less tuneful until at two o'clock in the morning everyone was complaining of a dry throat and clamouring for tea again.

'Well,' said Yawn, as we all relaxed for tea drinking. 'I'm thinkin' it's a good thing you got over all those colds and fever you had when you was tryin' to lift those stones. We wouldn't be after havin' such a good ceilidh as this one.' 'It was the first allusion he had made to my having been observed defying his warning.

231

'I've left them now, anyway,' I admitted ruefully.

'You should never have touched them at all,' reiterated Yawn, 'for you went to look real poorly after it.'

'Indeed so she did,' agreed Morag. 'I didn't like the look of you at all,' she said to me.

'Ach, I don't believe myself it was anythin' to do with the fever,' put in Behag with surprising conviction. 'I think Miss Peckwitt just got herself a good cold and that was the start of it all, likely.'

The old men shook their heads, knowingly.

'Ach, these colds,' grumbled Ian. 'I never had no trouble with all this catarrh an' sinuses as the doctor says I have until I started to use a handkerchief.' He darted a lugubrious glance at his sister, a very refined lady, who was sometimes to be heard chiding him for not using one. 'It's my belief it's handkerchiefs that's the cause of all these colds that are going about nowadays,' he said.

'Anyway,' interjected Morag, evidently deciding there had been enough censure for the time being, 'Miss Peckwitt's all right now, are you not?' She turned to me for confirmation.

'More or less,' I replied. 'I'm still having trouble with my chest, though. It's pretty uncomfortable at times.'

'Well then,' commented Erchy 'You know what you must do for that?'

'No,' I said, hurriedly trying to recollect some of the old cures about which I had heard from time to time during my residence in Bruach. 'What should I do?'

'You should get yourself a bottle of Stallion Mixture

and rub yourself with it. It's the finest thing in the world for bad chests.'

'Stallion Mixture?' I echoed blankly, and one of the girls giggled.

'What would Miss Peckwitt be wantin' with Stallion Mixture?' demanded Morag, indignant on my behalf. 'It's her chest that's troublin' her not her horse.'

'I know that fine,' retorted Erchy. 'But you mind my cousin Ruari had awful trouble with his own chest? He tried everythin' for it just, until he found he had a bottle of Stallion Mixture left in the house from when his horse was sick. He rubbed himself with that every day for a week an' he's never had a spot more trouble since.' He turned to me. 'You should get a bottle from the grocer tomorrow,' he urged me. 'That'll see your bad chest off for you.'

'I shouldn't like to risk rubbing myself with Stallion Mixture,' I told him, smiling.

'What's the risk?' he demanded. 'It never did my cousin any harm. Indeed,' he resumed with increasing enthusiasm, 'you should have seen the way the hair grew on his chest with the stuff. Just like a Highland bull he was, an' he fathered three fine sons after it.'

'Surely it must have dribbled a bit, then,' observed the irrepressible Morag, while several of the girls shrieked with coy appreciation.

Yawn stood up stiffly. 'I'm away home to my bed,' he said, and there was a murmur of assent from the rest of the old folk that the younger people affected not to hear.

'I'm sure Miss Peckwitt must be tired,' announced Katy,

with a solicitousness that was belied by the mockery of her smile.

'I am,' I admitted unashamedly, well accustomed by now to being teased about my habit of liking to go to bed on the same day as I got up. There was a general if reluctant movement to go, the old folk saying good night with seeming abruptness as they were met by the icy air that came in through the open door. Apparently impervious to the cold the lassies clustered round the doorway waiting for the men to arouse themselves from the alcoholic drowsiness into which they had fallen. Becoming impatient, they grasped the men bodily and pulled them to their feet and together they all stumbled out into the night, singing and arguing their way along the road into the darkness. I waited only to tidy the room before going to bed where I fell into a deep and contented sleep from which I was aroused somewhere around six o'clock in the morning by the sound of the coal lorry being driven away.

'Well, I enjoyed my ceilidh fine last night,' said Morag, and then she went on to pay me the Hebridean's supreme compliment, 'I didn't feel the time passin'.'

'Good,' I replied.

'Was that the coal lorry I heard away at the back of six this mornin'?' she enquired.

'I believe it was. I wonder where he was until that time?'

'He'd be with Mora,' said Morag with complete certainty. 'My, but she's the one for the lads all right.' She made a disparaging noise in the back of her throat. 'You'll no' go short of coal for a while till she's tired of him,' she added.

'Well that's good to hear,' I said. We were nearing the entrance to my croft and Morag could now see the heap of coal the lorry had dumped. It looked pitifully small.

'Here, but that's surely not half a ton,' she declared.

'It's supposed to be,' I told her, though I too had been suspicious about the quantity when I saw it by daylight.

'It's never half a ton,' she insisted. 'You should tell him that when you see him next. You know how it is with these lads at the yard?'

I nodded. The loading of coal, unless it was being delivered direct from the boat, was a homely affair. As each half hundredweight of coal was decanted on to the lorry from a large scoop a stone was placed on a convenient windowsill and when there were twenty or forty stones on the sill there was considered to be half a ton or a ton of coal in the lorry. This method generally worked quite well but as the loading was rarely conducted with much seriousness on the part of the loaders it was not wholly reliable. Any distraction, such as an incipient dog fight, might be prevented by someone picking up a stone from the sill and hurling it at the combatants; or perhaps a wandering child, unnoticed by the loaders, would appropriate a couple of the more interesting-looking stones. In either case you got jolly good measure for your money but, as it was just as likely that the child might decide to add a few stones to the array on the windowsill or even that one of the ubiquitous loiterers would take an impish delight in surreptitiously adding a stone or two to confuse the loaders, your delivery of coal might be quite seriously short.

'I'll tell the driver about it next time I see him,' I said to Morag. 'And you'll be able to corroborate, won't you?'

'Indeed I will,' she promised.

It was only two evenings later, but well after dark, that the lorry driver turned up at the cottage.

'Morag's after tellin' me you got short weight with your coal,' he began.

'Yes, I'm sure I did,' I told him. 'I honestly don't think there was more than about six hundredweight in it. Here,' I handed him my big torch, 'go and have a look for yourself.'

He went, and came back sucking his breath disapprovingly. 'I was kind of thinkin' that it was short myself at the time,' he acknowledged. 'I suppose it was the lads got larkin' about. I was takin' my tea at the time.' There was a deep frown between his eyes and he seemed a little uncertain what to say next. I asked him inside for a cup of tea but he refused it hastily. 'I'll tell you what I'll do,' he said, making up his mind. 'If you'll take another half-ton of coal I'll load it myself and see there's extra put on to make up for last time.'

As I have said, coal had been in short supply for some time and the prospect of another half-ton was extremely attractive. 'Of course I'll take it,' I told him, unable to disguise my eagerness.

'Right, then, I'll try will I bring it out tomorrow.' He jumped into the lorry and drove off and, much to my amazement, about the same time the following evening I heard the lorry approaching and soon another load of coal was being added to the heap on my croft. The sight of it glistening in the light of the torch filled me with satisfaction.

'It's wonderful to have a nice stock of coal,' I said. 'I've had so many colds this year and I've found it impossible to keep warm with just peats no matter how high I build the fire.'

The driver looked sympathetic. 'How long d'you reckon it takes you to get through half a ton of coal?' he asked me.

I thought for a moment. 'About six weeks,' I told him.

'Then that lot you have will no' last you very long,' he pointed out. 'Twelve weeks at the most.'

'That's true,' I agreed.

'I'll not be makin' any promises but if I can get you more coal will you take it?' he asked.

'I'll be only too glad to,' I said rashly.

'Right then. Cheerio, I'll be seein' you,' he called and was away again, racing his lorry over the bumps of the road and leaving me to wonder why I had suddenly become such a favourite. It took Morag to put me wise.

'Didn't I tell you you'd get plenty coal after your ceilidh?' she asked. 'I could see then the way it was goin' to be between him and Mora.'

'Oh, I don't think it's just Mora who's bringing him out here so often with coal for me,' I said. 'I think he feels sorry for me because I've been so long without coal.'

Morag smiled compassionately at my ignorance. 'Sure it's Mora,' she averred. 'The only way he can get out to see her at night is on the lorry an' the only way he can get hold of the lorry is by sayin' he's bringin' folks coal. Indeed isn't he after everyone in the village swearin' that it's the hardest part of the winter to come yet.'

'Oh, I see,' I said. 'But,' I added brightly, 'good luck to him. I've told him I'll take all the coal he can bring me.'

'Maybe you'll be sorry yet, then,' she said, but I laughed her warning away. I could always use more coal, I told myself with a feeling of light-heartedness. In that way I differed from the rest of the crofters for they used little coal, some of them none at all, and they seemed to find all the warmth they needed in a few peats smouldering greyly in the grate, but then they wore much the same clothes indoors and outdoors, even leaving on their gumboots. I, who felt a slattern unless I changed when I had finished my outside chores, liked to stoke up the fire lavishly in the evenings so that I could move about the room without finding myself in a cold corner. I had told the lorry driver half a ton of coal lasted me about six weeks. Half a ton lasted most of the crofters a year or more.

The obliging driver turned up with another half-ton of coal the following week and within a few days there was yet another half-ton. Gloatingly I regarded the growing heap. My winter's supply of coal secured within easy reach of my cottage! The weather could do its worst now and I need not worry. I was extremely grateful to the driver. So much so that the following week I was confronted with yet another half-ton of coal. I began to feel faintly perturbed. Although I told myself it was a good idea to have a reserve of coal against the time when it might be unobtainable—a circumstance that was all too familiar in Bruach—I had to face up to the fact that coal cost money and my own resources were strictly limited. It was with dismay that I heard the coal lorry turn on to the croft the very next week and, like 'the sorcerer's apprentice', I began to wonder when the flow was going to stop.

'Look,' I told the driver, with affected joviality. 'I'll take up to five tons and then you must marry the girl or else give her up. I can't afford to buy anymore.'

He grinned self-consciously and when he bade me goodnight his voice was distinctly regretful.

'Here,' said Erchy some time later in the month. 'You want to be glad now you've plenty of coal. You'll not be gettin' any more for a while. That lorry driver's quarrelled with his boss so he's not workin' for him any more.'

I felt a sense of relief, which was shortlived for, not many evenings later I again heard a lorry approaching with a very familiar rumble and on going outside I found myself confronting my driver friend. My heart plunged to my boots.

'Not more coal?' I asked apprehensively.

'No, indeed,' he assured me. 'I've finished with that man.' He came into the kitchen and sat down uninvited. As he seemed prepared to stay for a while I offered him tea and as he drank it he described to me the various jobs he had tried. When he had finished his tea and was about to leave he asked, 'Did I no' hear you sayin' somethin' at the ceilidh about wantin' a new peat shed?'

'You might have heard me say that I was wanting to

strengthen the one I already have,' I told him.

'Aye, well, what I was thinkin' was, I'm workin' now for a fellow has good slabs of wood—you know, the outside of the trees, I'm meanin'. They're good and cheap and if I brought you a load out here in my spare time the carriage would cost you nothin' at all.'

He was an exceedingly persuasive young salesman. It seemed a good idea, and I fell for it. A load of slabs was soon delivered and Erchy went to work on the shed.

'You know,' the driver told me, 'you should take advantage of these slabs while they're so cheap and get yourself another load. You could build yourself another shed with them and make new stalls for your cow byre. There's no end to what you can do with them and you won't be able to get them for much longer.'

The stalls in the byre were sketchy indeed; I succumbed and ordered another load.

'Well,' said Morag, when she saw them lying on the croft. 'You only just got your slabs in time. He's quarrelled with the slab mannie, so he's not workin' for him any more.' She shook her head, lamenting upon the fickleness of the young driver.

'Who is he working for now, then?' I asked.

'Indeed, I'm hearin' he's gone to that place that's sellin' the lime,' she told me.

During my residence in Bruach the village had been visited by one expert after another, all sent by some official body to advise on methods of improving croft land. Lime, they had invariably insisted, was the basic and most urgent necessity. Lime, lime and lime again, they adjured us. The crofters were frankly disbelieving; lime cost money, so they preferred to retain their faith in dung and seaweed. I think I was the only person who accepted the findings of the experts at that time, so that when the lorry driver eventually presented himself at my door with the offer of a load of lime brought out at cheap rates in the evening I was not too unwilling to accept. He generously offered to help me spread the first load, an offer which, had I suspected the reason for it, I should not have accepted with so much alacrity. The experts had said two tons to the acre but the driver spread his share so prodigally that the ton he had brought out did not cover nearly half that area.

'Ach, but I'll be bringin' you out another ton tomorrow,' he comforted. 'You can't give this land too much lime,' he added with an air of superior knowledge.

'And anyway,' he added shrewdly, 'you'll want to qualify for the subsidy on it.'

We spread another ton the following night.

'You would be the better of twenty tons of lime on this croft,' the driver observed briskly flapping his overalls.

'I'm liming only two acres of it for a start,' I told him with a firmness that was no doubt accentuated by my chalk-white face. 'That means I'll need four tons altogether. I'm not taking any more than that.' But after he had brought me the third ton the deliveries ceased abruptly.

'I'm thinkin' you'll need to wait a good whiley for the rest of your guana,' Morag crowed. Everything used to fertilize the land that was not recognizable as seaweed or honest dung, Morag persisted in describing as 'guana'.

'Why?' I asked. 'Has he quarrelled with the lime merchant now?'

'Indeed he has,' she replied.

'Oh, well, I suppose he'll soon get a job with someone else and be out here again coaxing us to buy things at cheap rates.' I laughed.

Morag gave me an odd look. 'An' he's after finishin' with Mora, too,' she said.

'Really?' I exclaimed.

'Aye, so he has,' she told me. 'An' it's glad you ought to be for that, mo ghaoil, for the new job he has is with the undertaker.'

XII. *Ladies in Distress*

THE WOMAN IN THE BED next to mine swung her legs cautiously over the side while the nurse waited, holding her dressing-gown.

'They're letting me home on Friday,' she told me.

'Where is home?' I asked her and she described to me a little village, the name of which, along with many others, I had glimpsed so often in the *Oban Times*.

'Where's yours?' she asked, and when I told her she was immediately sympathetic. 'That's an awful way away,' she said. 'No wonder you don't get many visitors.'

My one and only visitor had come the previous evening and then it had been well past visiting hours. The evening meal had been served and there had been the usual period of comparative inactivity before we were bedded down for the night. The patients were meditative and only the rus-

tling of paper as presents were inspected and the light quick
footsteps of the nurses broke the lazy silence of the ward.
All at once we became aware of the heavy, unsure tread of
rough boots. Everyone turned to look at the tall, embarrassed man, clad in homespun suit and cloth cap, who stood
at the entrance. With a glow of pleasure I managed to lift
my arm in an attempt at a wave and he came towards my
bed, hesitantly at first and then with clumsy haste, his boots
skidding on the highly polished floor.

'Hector!' I said, and my eyes filled with tears. 'Hector,
this is wonderful.'

'Why, Miss Peckwitt,' he said, obviously dismayed at
my wasted appearance. 'I just couldn't believe it was you
till you spoke just. Oh dear, dear.' He shook his head and
looked so distressed that I had to smile reassuringly.

'I'm getting along fine,' I told him, though so far he
had been too overcome to ask how I was. 'But tell me, how
did you get here, Hector?'

'I heard the carrier was comin' wiss some sheeps tsis
way, so I said would he give me a lift and here I am.' He
gave me a rueful little smile. 'Behag said I was to get you
tsese.' He put a bag of fruit down on my bedside table. 'An'
I tsought maybe you'd like tsis.' He laid a copy of the *Foot-
ball Times* down on the bedcover.

'Tell me all the news,' I begged, when I had expressed
my pleasure over the gifts. He rubbed his hand over his
chin and frowned with concentration. After a few moments
the frown lifted.

'Tsere's a lot of people told me to tell you tsey was askin'' after you,' he said and reeled off a list of names. 'An' Morag said to tell you your cow and hens is doin' fine,' he finished up.

I nodded gratefully. 'And how is everyone in Bruach and what have they been doing?' I asked him.

'Ach, tsey're fine,' he said. 'An' tsey're just where tse tide left tsem when last you saw tsem. I don't know tsat tsey've been doin' anytsing at all.'

I had been in hospital for some weeks and even in Bruach I was sure something would have happened in that time. Surely someone had bought a new cow, or lost an old one. Or someone's hay had blown away or someone's horse had fallen over a cliff?

'Have the storms been very bad?' I prompted.

'Och, aye. Some of tsem. Daft Donald lost his dinghy in tse last one. Smashed up properly she was. Mind you, she was as rotten as shit.'

'Poor Donald,' I commiserated. 'He'll miss not having the *Swallow* to fuss over, even though he never went out in her.'

'Aye, but he has anotser one already,' Hector said. 'He got it from a man on tse mainland a few days ago just, an' he was round tse otser day askin' my aunt what name would he put on it.'

'And did she suggest one?'

'Aye, well all she said was, "What's wrong wiss callin' her *Swallow* again, Donald?" So tsats what he did. I was down on tse shore yesterday and tsere across tse transom of his boat he's painted *Swallow Again* in big letters.' He smiled a swift, urchin smile. 'It kind of gives you a funny feelin' in your tsroat just to see it,' he said, and we exchanged a grin of understanding.

'No cows died? No calves born?' I asked.

'No, but tse stallion was out tse otser day for Tearlaich's mare—tse one tsat didn't die. Tse mannie tsat brought him was sayin' he was pretty fed up, too.'

'Why?'

'He was girnin' because he'd had to walk all tse way from tse pier wiss tse beast an' he'd be after havin' to walk all tse way back again tsat night for tsere was no place to keep him.'

'I should think he would be fed up,' I murmured.

'Aye, well tse minute tse stallion had served tse mare tse mannie grabbed a great bunch of nettles an' rammed tsem under tse mare's tail. My God! he was quick about it too. An' he needed to be, for she kicked up her heels to witsin an inch of his head. "Tsere now," he says to Tearlaich an' givin' him a wink, "tsat'll make sure she holds an I don't have to come back here again." Tearlaich turns on him. "Man," he says, "you're lucky to be alive not to have to come back again."' Hector's eyes were wide. 'An' I can tell you he was, too.'

Hector had not taken off his cap when he came into the ward and now, becoming conscious of the questioning looks of the night nurses just coming on duty, he pulled it down over his eyes so that he should not see them.

'Has no one died or been ill?' I asked him.

He shook his head and sucked in his breath, trying to

remember something that might interest me.

'Hamish's sister is back,' he suddenly recalled.

'Is she really? Is she any better?'

Hamish's sister had developed, in addition to other peculiar habits, one of hiding behind any convenient shed or house whenever she saw anyone approaching and giving a very life-like imitation of a duck quacking. A few months ago she had been taken to a home to be treated.

Hector pondered my question. 'Well I don't know tsat she's better,' he said doubtfully. 'She's different tsough.'

'How different?'

'Well, she doesn't quack any more, but now whenever she sees you comin' she gets behind sometsing and crows away like a cockerel. She's damty good at it, too,' he said with an appreciative smile.

The nurse came to the foot of the bed and though Hector gave her his most enraptured smile she was not to be beguiled. He shrugged and cast a furtive glance along the rows of interested faces. I thought he was going to kiss me goodbye but his courage failed him. Instead he patted my hand.

'Never mind,' he said, 'you'll be better off for tsis operation, you'll see. Our own Hamish had an operation on his stomach at one time an' he never had any more trouble wiss it till he died.'

He lingered a moment or two longer. 'You'll be home for New Year?' he predicted questioningly, and when I shook my head he made a grimace of sympathy. I watched him with great affection as he skidded out of the ward and turned to wave to me before disappearing along the corridor. Then I lay back on the pillows, reflecting on his parting words.

Would I be home for New Year? Not, I planned, if I could help it. Out of hospital, I hoped, but not in Bruach where New Year was just a drinking orgy in which, because I loathe undisciplined drinking, I had perforce to play the part of observer. The first New Year I had spent there in Morag's house I had been so nauseated by the intemperance of the crofters that I had resolved when I got a house of my own I would withdraw completely from the celebration. Morag, who always had my interests at heart, had then made it her duty to come and explain to me how much New Year meant to them and how important it was that I should take a drink with my friends even if it was only a 'wee tastie'. I was never able to understand the Scots' preparatory bracing up for their complete abandonment to sottishness on this one night of the year but I was made to see how churlish and unsociable was my own attitude. So I had relented and bought a bottle of whisky and stayed up to entertain such revellers as were sober enough to stumble to my cottage. It was for me a long night of unmitigated boredom but since then I had become more acclimatized and had found that the best way of coping with the celebration was to set out myself just before midnight and go the rounds of my friends' houses taking my own bottle and wishing everyone a 'Happy New Year' and accepting only a 'wee tastie' in return. It still meant a long and tedious night but I preferred it to sitting at home and perhaps being surrounded by limp carcasses singing, praying, crying or just being horribly sick.

And yet, even at New Year, there were moments of fun. I remembered how it had been last year.

It had begun when 'postie' had burst into the cottage, decanted some very muddy envelopes on to the table and pulled a bottle of whisky out of his mailbag. His eyes were Hogmanay bright.

'It's a bugger of a night for a New Year,' he began sociably. 'The wind lifted the mails out of my bag just, an' it took them halfway up the brae before I could catch them again.' He paused for breath. 'Indeed I doubt I wouldn't have got them at all if they hadn't been caught in those bushes at the back of Sandy's house.' He bade me get two glasses and when I put them on the table he poured a generous quantity into each. He tossed off his at one gulp. 'I'll be seein' you again tonight yet,' he threatened as he girded his bag to him in preparation for the resumption of his battle against the storm. 'I'm goin' up to Erchy's when I've finished an' then we'll be startin' on the rounds.'

'Well don't leave it too late,' I warned him. 'I'm going up to Morag's before twelve.'

'Ach, we'll be there by then,' he promised.

I slammed the door after him and sagged into a chair. I had not been feeling too well for over a week and I really had no intention of going up to Morag's. I hoped that round about midnight there would be a quiet spell when I could put out the light and creep off to bed and let everyone think I was following my usual plan of having my New Year ceilidh in other people's houses. Throughout the evening there came a sporadic trickle of visitors coming and going in varying stages of inebriation. Whisky poured by crapulous hands was slopped on the table and on the floor and in the brief intervals between drinks the talk was senseless and repetitive.

At half past eleven the cottage was mercifully deserted and I was just about to put out the light and bolt the door when there was a peremptory knock on the window followed by a thump on the door and Morag came in.

'What, is there nobody here?' she asked, peering under the table and behind the chairs where she would expect to find New Year revellers. I told her who had come and gone. 'An' has our own Hector an' Erchy not been yet?' I shook my head. 'Well, I may as well sit myself down and wait till they do,' she announced, seating herself beside the fire, 'for they'll surely be here before the mornin'.'

I got out the bottle again and a couple of tots but she insisted that it must be 'only a wee tastie', just so that it could never be said she had refused to drink with me. The women of Bruach rarely took more to drink than they needed just to make themselves merry. It was only the men who insisted on quantity. We sat and talked until two o'clock and still there was no sound of approaching 'first footers'.

'It's a pity you don't take to New Year like the rest of us,' said Morag. 'Did you never make anythin' of it when you was in England?'

'Not really,' I told her. 'We had all our fun at Christmas.' I smiled reminiscently. 'The only difference New Year made at home was that my father used to stay up to let the

New Year in and he used to have a bottle of wine and a cigar for company.'

'A cigar! There now.' Morag was visibly impressed.

'Yes,' I said. 'My mother used to buy him two three-and-sixpenny cigars for Christmas every year and he smoked one on Christmas day and one on New Year's Eve.'

'Three and sixpence for one cigar?' expostulated Morag. 'That seems a terrible waste of money.'

'Oh, no,' I replied. 'It was only two in the whole year. The rest of the time he smoked a pipe.'

'The dear Lord help us!' responded Morag fervently. 'If I paid three and sixpence for a cigar for a man I'd be after makin' sure he ate the ash of it.'

Even the small amount of whisky I had drunk was making me sleepy and I was unable to suppress my yawns. Morag too seemed to be a little tired. The clock struck three.

'I was thinkin' maybe Erchy wouldn't have all that much money to spend on drink after him losin' so much this week already,' Morag said.

'Erchy losing his money?' I asked. 'That's the first I've heard of it. How did that happen?' My sleepiness was temporarily abated.

'Did you not hear? He went off on Monday to the mainland with some of his beasts he was takin' to a sale there, an' Hector was supposed to be goin' with him. Erchy went on the cattle float, but our own Hector—ach! you know what like of man he is.' She made a gesture of hopelessness with her hands. 'Didn't he tell Erchy he'd meet him at the ferry because he was gettin' a lift in with the nurse in the mornin' to go and see the blacksmith about a thing for his boat. Well, he goes to see the blacksmith an' then he's outside waitin' on the bus to take him to the ferry when a car pulls up beside him. "You're Hector, aren't you, from Bruach?" says the driver. "I've met you before when I took a trip on your boat." Hector just can't remember his face but the man asks him would he like a lift. So Hector gets in, well pleased with himself.' Morag gave a dry chuckle. 'My, but he got a right drop when the car turns round an' comes back here to Bruach.'

'But didn't Hector say anything when he saw which way it was going?' I asked.

'Indeed he did not. The fool said he didn't like to when the mannie had been so kind to him.'

Hector was so afraid of hurting anyone's feelings that I sometimes used to amuse myself by imagining him driving a car on a busy road. I used to feel sure that if he received a polite 'pass' signal from the car in front he would, sooner than appear discourteous, obediently overtake even though doing so would mean that he would drive straight past the turning for his own destination.

'Anyway,' Morag resumed. 'Hector didn't get to the sale so Erchy was there by himself an' he made two hundred pounds on his beasts. Of course, Erchy bein' who he is, he had to go an' get drunk an' when he wakes up it's mornin' an' he's cold an' shiverin' in the waitin' room of the station. He puts his hand in his pocket an' there's his wallet missin'. All his cattle money's gone.'

'Poor Erchy,' I said. 'Whatever did he do?'

'That's not the end of it,' said Morag. 'He has to go an borrow a pound or so from a man he knows to get him home.' I watched her avidly, waiting for the climax which I knew by her manner I could expect.

'Ach, the way poor Erchy was feelin' an' havin' to face his mother an tellin' her what he'd done! An' the poor old soul hearin' him!'

'And is there no trace of the wallet?' I asked.

'Well, comes twelve o'clock,' went on Morag, nodding me into silence, 'an' what should draw up outside Erchy's house but a taxi. An' what does this taxi do next but to start unloadin' parcels of groceries an' cakes that the driver gives to Erchy.

' "Here's the messages you ordered," the driver tells him. "Oh, God!" says Erchy, frettin' about what other foolishness he might have been up to. "Did I order these?" For he has no mind of it at all. "You did indeed," the driver says, quite sharp. "An' you ordered my taxi to bring them out here to you at twelve o'clock today." "An' how much did I pay you for doin' it?" Erchy asks him. "You didn't pay me," says the driver. "You promised you'd pay me two pounds ten if I brought them all to you safely at twelve o'clock today, an' there's the sheet of paper where you wrote down your name an' address." Erchy looks at the paper an' there's no mistake about it at all. He's just swearin' off the drink for the rest of his life when the driver pulls out a wallet an' hands it to him. "An' there's your wallet you asked me to keep for you," he said. "You'd best check what's in it. A hundred and ninety-five pounds you told me it was last night so it should be the same now." Erchy could scarce believe his ears an' he takes the wallet an' looks in it, an' there's a hundred an' ninety-five pounds.' Morag finished with an exclamation of incredulity.

'Oh good! So he didn't lose his money after all,' I said with as much relief as if it had been mine.

'None but twenty pounds of it,' said Morag. I raised my eyebrows enquiringly and she carried on with her story.

'"Now," says the driver, "I'd be glad if you'll pay me an' I can get back."

'"How much did you say I promised to pay you?" Erchy asked.

'"Two pounds ten," said the driver, thinkin' Erchy was goin' to argue.

'"Man," says Erchy, "I'm that damty glad to see you I'll give you twenty-two pounds ten!" An' he made the driver take it, too.'

'My goodness! I'll bet Erchy said his prayers after that little lot,' I said.

'Maybe he's still celebratin' his luck,' she said, standing up. 'I'm thinkin' the best thing we can do is to go and find out where he and that Hector are, anyway,' she suggested. 'They're sure to be somewhere if it's only the ditch they're in. But there's one thing certain, mo ghaoil, if you don't have a drink with them some place tonight then there's no use in you goin' to bed for they'll be here yet an' get you out of it, no matter what time it is.'

So instead of seeking my warm bed I had put on oil-skins and gumboots and blundered with Morag out into the rumbustious night. We had called and taken our 'wee tastie' in several houses before we finally caught up with Erchy and his crowd at Dugald's cottage and there men were sprawled all over the kitchen, some with their heads on the shoulders of the long-suffering girls who, though it was past four o'clock in the morning and they had been celebrating since early evening, were as dewy-eyed and fresh-looking as if they had just come in from the hill. The Highland complexion has never, to me, ceased to be a source of envy and wonder. Dugald himself sat on the bench buttressed on either side by his chief cronies while in the recess bed behind drawn curtains his stone-deaf wife alternately snored and screeched objurgations at the assembled company. There was an ominous belch from the floor by the dresser and a frenzy of catarrhal sobs interspersed with protestations of remorse for his misdeeds came from Tearlaich, whose religion made him very conscious of the fact that he often sinned but never stopped him from doing so. Hector lurched over and waved a bottle of whisky over an empty glass which he pushed in my direction. With great solemnity we wished each other a happy New Year. Then it was Erchy's turn and then Ruari's and so on until they were all satisfied that they had poured me out a drink and had seen me raise the glass to my lips. Dugald attempted a song but before one line was completed his head had sunk on his chest and he was sagging with sleepiness.

I was assessing my chances of making a stealthy retreat when I found Erchy teetering over me.

'Your hair smells lovely of boiled onions,' he remarked

with an ardent sniff, and without giving me time to accept his compliment he went on, 'Miss Peckwitt, I want you to help me.'

I indicated that I was quite willing to help him if I could.

'It's this Dugald here. He's that drunk an' somebody's got to get him home tonight,' he explained. He swayed sideways and steadied himself against the back of my chair. 'I'm thinkin' you an' me are the only two here that's sober enough to be any good to him.' I suppose I looked as mystified as I felt. 'Come on, now,' he invited. 'I daresay we can manage him between us.'

'But, Erchy,' I remonstrated, 'this is Dugald's house. He's in his own home.'

Erchy recoiled from me with a look of anguished incredulity. 'Woman!' he upbraided me, 'you must be bloody drunk if that's what you're thinkin'.' He shook Morag's shoulder. 'You'd best get this woman to her bed,' he adjured her, 'for she's that drunk she doesn't know where she is.'

And the next day, looking like something the mice had been nibbling at during the night, he had come quite early down to the cottage to commiserate with me on my 'sore head'.

The woman in the next bed said: 'It's wonderful to think I'll be sleeping in my own room again on Friday night—and I won't have to wake up in a morning and see all those memorial tablets over the beds. They fair give me the creeps.'

I agreed most heartily with her, for it is disturbing and disheartening to come out of an anaesthetic with one's body a tangle of pain to be confronted by a well-polished but sombre plaque stating that one's bed is dedicated to the memory of a deceased relative by a loving family. Seen vaguely, in conjunction with massed flowers and the white draperies of the nurses, the plaques give one the feeling that one is attending one's own funeral.

'It'd be far better if they had a few pictures over the beds instead of those things,' said my neighbour. 'The adventures of Tarzan all along the walls would do more to cheer us women up than a lot of old memorials.'

'It's pretty awful psychology, I should think,' I said. 'And I'm sure a few delectable pin-ups would benefit the men's ward.'

She laughed. 'Ach, well, you've done your little bit, anyway, dearie.' She laughed again and I darted her a look of venom while every nerve in my body cringed with embarrassment.

'Your blessed brother-in-law,' I commented.

I had been lying stark-naked on my bed under the infra-red lamp the previous day and though the screens were around me the nurse had left a gap so that I could watch the ward clock and call her when my cooking was completed. I was basking contentedly in the soothing heat from the lamp and so paid little attention to the tall man in a dressing-gown who had just come into the ward and was talking to the nurse. I had not taken particular notice when, guided by her pointing finger, he made his way along the line of beds in my direction and it was not until a second or two before he reached my bed that I realized his proximity.

Immobilized by an intravenous feeder and in any case too weak to move quickly I could only stare with agonized horror as he leaned his arms on my screens and greeted me with startled affability. I screwed my eyes tight shut and a moment later heard my neighbour's voice lifted in rebuke.

'Andrew! This is me over here.'

His head had disappeared by the time I could endure to open my eyes again and there was much awed whispering from the direction of the next bed. When he had gone and, my cooking over, I was settled beneath the bedclothes again, my neighbour called to me. 'That was my brother-in-law. Seemingly they brought him into the men's ward yesterday for an X-ray.'

'I don't care if he is your brother-in-law,' I stated flatly. 'He's a blundering oaf.'

She laughed with irritating complacency. 'He just made a mistake in thinking the nurse was pointing to your bed,' she excused him. 'But he told me to tell you he was awful sorry for coming on you like that.' She tried hard to look solemn.

'I feel so ashamed,' I grumbled. 'And I shall always be dreading the possibility that I may meet him again somewhere. Imagine how I shall feel if I ever come face to face with a complete stranger who's seen me in my birthday suit.'

'Ach, but you have no need to worry, dearie. He'll never recognize you.'

'I sincerely hope not,' I said.

'Oh, no, he won't honestly,' she assured me with artful positiveness. 'He told me he didn't bother to look at your face.'

On Thursday evening my neighbour sat on my bed and chatted with me for as long as the nurse would allow. I always thought of her as 'Rosie' because her offhand geniality, her voluptuous figure and her habit of calling everyone 'dearie' made me think of a typical English barmaid. In fact she was the postmistress of a village that, when she described it, sounded to me to be only a little more sophisticated than Bruach. Speaking of her own illness she said: 'My man was saying he didn't believe they would have needed to keep me so long in here had we been able to get the doctor when I first felt ill. But it's the same every year in our village.' She gave a sigh of resignation. 'It's no use wanting the doctor once the grouse-shooting season's begun for he's always too busy.' She fed me a segment of orange. 'You know, people never like to make a complaint against the doctor,' she said. 'There are doctors in the Highlands can get away with murder and people wouldn't say a word against them. The last doctor we had was asked to go to a man once that was sick and he promised to go but he forgot all about it. A few days later he was passing the house and he sees there's a funeral. He suddenly remembers the sick man and gets out of his car to ask after him. He finds it's the very man they're burying, so he just follows behind the bier to the burial ground. Afterwards all the relatives were saying, "Ach, there we were mis-calling the poor doctor for not coming out to visit the man but it seems he's not so bad after all. He did come to the funeral"'

'We're luckier than that where I live,' I told her. 'But I do remember one doctor we had who loved to buy cattle. If he saw a nice-looking beast anywhere along the road he couldn't rest until he'd found the owner and bargained with him for the cow. It would take hours sometimes and it didn't matter at all if he was supposed to be going to an urgent case.'

'Rosie' got up. 'Oh, well, I suppose I'd best get to my bed. The morning will come all the quicker for it.'

'What time is the ambulance to take you?' I enquired.

'Ambulance? I'm having no ambulance,' she asserted. 'My man's hiring a car for me since he heard what happened to the last woman from our village that was supposed to be sent home by ambulance.'

'Did it break down?' I asked.

'No, oh, no! But the woman said she was greatly taken with the way the ambulance driver kept turning round to ask her if she was feeling all right. She kept telling him she was fine. Then he said would she like a cup of tea at the next hotel they'd pass. She told him she would, so he took her inside and bought a nice tea for her. Then she got back into the ambulance and they started off again and when they were about half way home the driver asked her again if she was sure she felt all right. So she told him again she still felt fine. "In that case," he asked her, "would you mind going home by train for the rest of the way and I'll pay your fare for you?" She looked at him wondering what was the matter with him and he said, "You see, I have a girl friend lives just about here and if you'll go home by train I can go and spend the time at her house before I have to get back to the hospital."'

'And did she go home by train?'

'Oh, yes. She didn't like to say no, seeing as he'd bought her tea, but my man says he's not taking the risk of it happening to me.' She was climbing into bed as she finished her story and there was a crackling of paper as she commenced her supper of biscuits, for 'Rosie's' large appetite was not to be satisfied with hospital rations.

The lights in the ward were dimmed and when I had managed to wriggle my poor bottom, that was punctured like a sieve with injections, into the least agonizing position, I drowsed first into the short segments of dreams that precede sleep and then into the drugged doze from which I was awakened well before five in the morning so that my bed could be made. More than at any other time this early-morning eruption into activity, just when sleep was deepest, made me yearn for my own bed and the lazy, undemanding winter dawns in Bruach.

When morning came 'Rosie' was claimed by a smugly delighted husband and a gently fussing sister and her bed was soon occupied by a little girl who reminded me so much of Fiona that, except for the colour of hair, they might have been one and the same person. She was just as perverse, just as imperious and before she had been in the hospital more than a few hours she had acquainted herself with the complete genealogies of every nurse and every patient in the ward.

The long days dragged increasingly in proportion as my recovery speeded up. Each morning the surgeons, anonymous in their white coats, came and smiled down at me with cool, detached smiles and prodded my body with deft fingers. They applied stethoscopes to my stomach that was as bloated as a Botticelli angel's and congratulated me solemnly on its reboant rumblings. When I was not asleep I lay and listened to it with the same sort of clinical satisfaction and when, thinking to amuse myself, I put a piece of toilet paper (stamped 'Government property') over a comb and started to play it, it was some time before the rest of the patients in the ward realized that the noise I was making was intentional. And when a storm came out of a ragged sky, bullying the tall trees in the hospital grounds and rattling the ward windows, it was some consolation to know that all the wind in the world wasn't inside my stomach as in moments of agony I was willing to believe.

At last my own day for leaving came, but it was only to go on to a convalescent home and there I spent a blessedly sober New Year.

Morag had a fire going and my cottage warm and bright with welcome when I returned at last to Bruach and the overwhelming kindness of my neighbours.

'Did they tell you what was wrong with you?' Morag asked at last. 'We were told you were very poorly but nobody rightly seemed to know what it was.'

'I don't know myself,' I replied. 'They weren't very forthcoming at the hospital.'

So a few weeks later when the nurse called I asked her if she knew what had been wrong with me.

'All they told me was that you were terribly constricted and it was a very big operation,' she replied.

'I wonder just what that means?' I asked, but she shrugged her shoulders.

It was not long after my conversation with the nurse that I met Hector and Erchy coming up from the shore with paint brushes and scrapers in their hands and looking as though they had put in a full day's work. 'We've had *Ealasaid* up on the beach,' they told me in reply to my glance of enquiry.

'Why, was there something wrong with her?' I asked.

'Och, aye, she was terrible constricted.'

'Constricted?' I repeated, almost choking on the word. 'How do you mean?'

'It means she had a terrible dirty bottom,' elucidated Hector. 'Covered all over wiss weeds and tsem big barnacles. It's days we've been now scrapin' tsem off her and scrubbin' at her. It's been a right big job we've had wiss her.'

'And is she all right now?' I quavered, stifling the wild laughter that was threatening to shatter me.

'All right?' repeated Erchy. 'I'll say she's all right. Just you wait till you see her gettin' goin' again. You'll hardly know her she'll be that much faster.'

I too am a lot faster now.

Epilogue

THE MORNING WAS COLD and when my companion and I pushed open the door of the station waiting-room and saw the enormous fire we turned and stared at each other in joy and amazement. We rushed to crouch in front of it and were just beginning to feel our chilled bodies responding to the warmth when the door banged open and an overalled man came in brandishing a long-handled shovel. He gave us a perfunctory greeting and then, walking up to the fire he lunged at it with his shovel and lifted off most of the burning coals.

'Hey!' we reproached him testily. 'Why are you doing that?'

'I need it to light my engine,' he informed us with great dignity. 'You'll be wantin' the train to start, won't you?' The door slammed behind him.

My companion grinned. 'A real Highland farewell for you,' was his comment.

We huddled over the few coals left in the grate until a disgustingly cheerful porter came in and covered them with a shovelful of dross. I took a flask out of my bag and put it along with a packet of bread and butter and some hard-boiled eggs on the grimy table.

'The last of your own eggs?' queried my companion.

'Yes,' I admitted with a sad smile.

'I hope you're not going to miss having your own produce,' he remarked.

'Of course I shall miss it,' I told him. 'But not so much as I shall miss the people.'

'And the scenery?' he enquired.

'And the scenery.'

'And the rain and the gales and the midges?'

I shuddered. 'Not the midges.'

'You're not likely to be travelling on buses where the driver takes a ferret or a gun and invites the passengers to come and help him get a rabbit,' he warned.

'No,' I agreed. 'Nor where it's permissible to relieve a dull night journey by putting the headlights full on people so as to watch them fall into the ditch.' I chuckled in spite of my gloom.

'What would you be planning to do tomorrow if you were going back to Bruach?' asked my companion.

I thought for a moment. 'If the Lord spared me,' I began, and he giggled. 'I should probably be starting to dig for potatoes.' Immediately I said it I smelled the new-turned earth and saw the finished lazy beds looking like a tray of overdone sausage rolls.

'And you'd end the day with a backache!'

'Oh surely,' I affirmed. 'If the Lord spared me.'

'You won't be hearing that expression used where you're going.'

'I once heard Morag say, "I believe the poor man will die tonight surely," and then she added automatically, "if the Lord spares him."' We both giggled. 'I remember old Sarah telling me once, "Miss Peckwitt, if I was to die in the workhouse I don't believe I'd ever live down the shame of it."' The memories came crowding back as we ate in silence for a few minutes.

'I'm glad Bonny's gone to a good home,' I said. 'It was an awful wrench parting with her.'

'And your hens? You're satisfied about them?'

'Oh, yes!'

Janet had taken my hens although only a couple of months previously she and her brother had sworn to give up poultry-keeping altogether because it was too much trouble to confine the hens and, if they were allowed to roam, there were too many complaints from neighbours. So they had started to kill off and eat two hens each week and this had continued until there was only one hen left. Then Janet's brother had struck. 'I'm scunnered of killin' the poor things,' he had complained. 'An' I'm scunnered of eatin' them anyway, an' I'm damty sure this last one has got so tame I haven't the heart to kill the beast.'

'What will we do with her then?' Janet had asked him.

'It's no use keepin' one hen. She'll only get lonely and go off layin'.'

'Aye, well in that case we'll have some more to keep her company,' her brother had said and so my own offer had come just at the right time. It was such a typically Bruach incident that remembering it brought a warm glow of amusement.

'It wasn't Janet's brother who shot all the hens, was it?' my companion asked.

'No, that was another man. He'd always hated seeing the hens round the house but they belonged to his mother. He didn't dare do anything about them while she was alive because he believed she'd got a nice little nest egg put away and if he upset her she'd probably leave it to someone else. Anyway the morning after she was buried he stationed himself outside the little pop-hole of the hen house where the hens come out and he shot each one of them as it appeared.' I grimaced. 'He wasn't much liked in the village. Even Morag found it difficult to say a good word for him.'

My companion looked at me enquiringly.

'He was supposed to have fathered a child on a friend of hers but the girl's father refused to let her marry him even so. The poor girl died in childbirth and on the day of the funeral this man got out his bagpipes and marched round and round the father's croft playing jigs. He was touched, I think,' I added.

There were sounds of increasing activity on the station and we opened the door of the waiting-room to look out. There was still some time before the train would leave and the compartments would be cold still.

'You're going to miss Morag,' said my companion as we sat down again.

'Morag and Behag and Hector and Erchy. I'm going to miss them all terribly. Oh, and Murdoch and Janet and the postie—even little Fiona.'

'And that man with the thatch of red hair who was always saying rude things to everybody?'

'Oh, him!' I exclaimed. 'Yes, I shall miss him, too.' I remembered something. 'Did I ever tell you about the stuff he gave me to put on my hair?' My companion looked blank. 'I'd been grumbling to him that my hair was coming out in handfuls on the comb,' I explained, 'and he suddenly dashed off into his house and brought out a bottle of stuff which he urged me to use. He told me that many years ago, when he was working on a ship, his own hair had started to fall out. The ship had chanced to call at some little place in Portugal and there, very worried by now, he'd decided to go and find a chemist to see if he could get something to cure it. The chemist had had no English but had seemed to understand his complaint, and had given him a bottle of lotion which he had indicated he should rub into his scalp morning and evening. In a couple of weeks his hair had stopped falling out and was growing thicker and stronger than ever before. His shipmates had been very impressed and when the ship had called in the little port on her return journey they had all trooped up to the chemist and laid in a stock of this wonderful hair lotion.'

'Did you use it?'

'No,' I said. 'After the Stallion Mixture I was a bit suspicious. I was glad I hadn't too when a friend of Mary's came and translated the instructions for me—they were in Portuguese, of course. It turned out to be "a certain cure for mange in cats and dogs and other fur-bearing animals".'

'His own hair was a jolly good recommendation for it,' chuckled my companion.

'It was that same man who told me about an aunt of Janet's who used to brew whisky in her shebbeen long after it was made illegal,' I resumed when we had stowed our luggage and were settled in the compartment. 'Actually she was still alive when I first went to Bruach and I've never met a jollier old soul. She was always chock-full of impishness even at eighty-two.'

'Did she never get caught by the authorities?'

'Not actually caught,' I replied. 'The customs man came out one day supposedly to investigate but really he was more keen to go fishing so of course someone obliged with a boat and a crew and they kept him out a good while longer than he intended. When he came ashore he told one of the crew: "Go you and get a good dram for me from Janet's aunt. Tell her I'm near freezin' to death and just make her give it to you, whatever she says."'

'And what happened?'

'He got his dram all right but Janet's aunt got such a fright she went straight out and dumped the still and the rest of the stuff down what's reputed in Bruach to be a bottomless well, and she never attempted to make a drop of whisky again. The old folks have never really ceased to grumble about it. They say it was "good wild stuff" and only threepence a pint.'

'You haven't told me these stories before,' grumbled my companion.

I smiled. 'My diaries are full of them,' I confessed. 'Life in Bruach was crammed with similar incidents. When I'm feeling at all gloomy in the future I shall get them out and read through them to cheer myself up.'

'Why not write another book about them?' my companion suggested.

'No,' I replied. 'I don't think I shall write another book about Bruach.'

The guard's whistle shrilled long and loud. The engine blew out a triumphant hiss of pilfered steam. The train braced itself for the journey.